and before claiming to say something significant, they need to engage endless books, dissertations and articles, humbly listen to what others have said earlier, and with some guidance from supervisor and librarian, find their place at the academic discussion banquet. My heartfelt thanks to the authors of the book for reminding us of this so skillfully, multifacetedly, and generously.

Roman Soloviy
Director, Eastern European Institute of Theology (in partnership with EAAA)
Consultant to the Board of the Euro-Asian Accrediting Association

Best Practice Guidelines for Theological Libraries Serving Doctoral Students is a key contribution for any school in the Majority World. Its significance lies in the premise on which the whole book stands – that the library plays an indispensable role in any program, but especially in doctoral programs. *Best Practice Guidelines* demystifies the notion of the library's task as "book storage" by creating a holistic vision of a library system that functions as the cornerstone of the doctoral program and the institution. What I find extremely intriguing in the book is that it portrays the library as part of the institution's research culture, especially when having a doctoral program in place. The library, according to *Best Practice Guidelines*, is the main pillar on which the whole academic matrix rests safely.

Walid Zailaa
Academic Dean and Head Librarian,
Arab Baptist Theological Seminary, Beirut, Lebanon
Member, Middle East and North Africa Association for Theological Education (MENATE)

This is an important guide. It is well-structured and guided by a clear presentation of sixteen principles that are important for serving doctoral students. Based on my experiences as head librarian and research coordinator, as well as president of numerous associations and consultative bodies, I believe that the principles deserve an even stronger wording! I would especially like to stress two of the principles that are in the book:

> Principle #1: A doctoral program that is designed without regard to what the library and library personnel can offer is doomed to failure.

> Principle #4: Networking, networking, networking! When even Harvard is not able to buy all materials needed for their researchers, then a Majority World theological library will never make it without the help of colleagues at home and abroad.

Taking these principles into account will save a program a lot of money and frustration.

Geert Harmany
President, Bibliothèques Européennes de Théologie,
Head Librarian and Research Coordinator, Kampen University, Netherlands

As a person who has been involved in the Doctoral Initiative Steering Committee from the outset, I can confirm that *Best Practice Guidelines for Theological Libraries Serving Doctoral Programs* is a most unique and useful contribution to theological schools. This book considers various persons related to PhD programs, whether they are at the beginning of their journey or already established to a certain degree. We agree that a library is a key to the success of PhD programs, but equipping libraries requires significant time and effort, not to mention financial resources and staff expertise. This book projects and is prepared to deal with two seemingly asynchronous goals – good *and* affordable libraries for theological schools in the Majority World. This book is full of practical and adaptable examples and suggestions by specialist professionals, and it also provides step-by-step guidelines that any school can easily follow to create or upgrade its library in order to efficiently respond to the needs of its PhD program.

Jung-Sook Lee
Vice Chairperson, Asia Theological Association
Professor of Church History and former President,
Torch Trinity Graduate University, Seoul, Korea

The challenges of providing quality, doctoral level, theological education in the Majority World are well known. A doctorate is by definition a research degree. Research requires both professionally managed collections and professional research assistance. The costs of meeting these requirements in developing nations can seem prohibitive.

This timely and important work acknowledges the professional, economic, and administrative challenges facing theological educators in nations under pressure, but chooses to focus on solutions rather than problems. This creative, insightful volume provides sophisticated, nuanced and realistic guidance for administrators, librarians and other advocates who are trying to address the information needs of graduate students and scholars in the Majority World.

This volume, written by thoughtful and reflective professionals, provides indispensable direction for those who will educate the next generation of pastors, scholars and theologians.

Thomas E. Phillips
Director, Digital Theological Library,
Open Access Digital Theological Library, and Global Digital Theological Library

This comprehensive book on principles for theological libraries fills the need for guidelines in the evaluation, planning, and implementation of effective practices so theological libraries can better support good quality doctoral programs and their students, especially in the majority world. It points to the organic and fundamental interaction between library and curriculum in doctoral programs, and emphasizes important administrative aspects that must not be overlooked so the library can serve the research needs of students and faculty. The case studies of libraries in Africa, Asia and Europe illustrate the importance of the principles shared in the book.

This is a must-read for librarians, administrators, and accreditation officers in theological schools of the Majority World.

Elisabeth Sendek
Former President,
Seminario Bíblico de Colombia, Medellín, Columbia

Theological research, especially at the doctoral level, is never self-sufficient. In any theological project, we enter into a conversation that began long before us by representatives of different epochs, traditions of faith, theological schools, and denominations. As doctoral students cross the library threshold,

ICETE Series

Best Practice Guidelines for Theological Libraries Serving Doctoral Programs

ICETE

Global Hub for Evangelical Theological Education

Langham

GLOBAL LIBRARY

Best Practice Guidelines for Theological Libraries Serving Doctoral Programs

General Editor

Katharina Penner

Series Editors

Riad Kassis
Michael A. Ortiz

ICETE
Global Hub for Evangelical Theological Education

Langham
GLOBAL LIBRARY

Published 2021 by Langham Global Library
An imprint of Langham Publishing
www.langhampublishing.org

Langham Publishing and its imprints are a ministry of Langham Partnership

Langham Partnership
PO Box 296, Carlisle, Cumbria, CA3 9WZ, UK
www.langham.org

ISBNs:
978-1-83973-602-5 Print
978-1-83973-609-4 ePub
978-1-83973-611-7 PDF

British Library Cataloguing-in-Publication Data
A catalogue record for this book is available from the British Library

ISBN: 978-1-83973-602-5

Cover & Book Design: projectluz.com

Contents

Foreword. xi

Introduction. 1

Part I: Principles for Best Library Practice 5

Area 1: Integration of Library in Planning a Doctoral Program 5
  Principle #1: The library prominently participates in the preparation
    of the doctoral program   5
  Principle #2: The library prioritizes the unique needs of doctoral
    students and assigns personnel for the doctoral program   7

Area 2: Partnerships and Collaboration. 9
  Principle #3: The library collaborates with faculty in
    research-related areas   9
  Principle #4: The library collaborates with other libraries locally
    and internationally   11

Area 3: Collection Development and Management. 12
  Principle #5: The library's collection serves the curriculum, including
    the doctoral program   12
  Principle #6: Collection development and management are governed
    by policy   13
  Principle #7: The collection development policy emphasizes
    acquisition for the doctoral program   14
  Principle #8: The library provides access to print and electronic
    resources   14
  Principle #9: The library fosters accessibility and sharing through a
    recognized classification system and online catalogue   17

Area 4: The Role(s) of Library Personnel. 17
  Principle #10: The institution has sufficient qualified library staff   18
  Principle #11: Library staff consistently emphasize a "service culture"
    and continuously improve their user-orientation   19
  Principle #12: Library staff are continuously involved in life-long
    learning and professional development   20

Area 5: Information Literacy in Doctoral Program(s)................ 21

    Principle #13: The library develops an Information Literacy policy
    and curriculum 22

    Principle #14: The library provides initial and ongoing orientation
    for doctoral students 23

    Principle #15: Librarians collaborate with faculty in Information
    Literacy interventions 24

    Principle #16: The library is part of the institution's research culture ... 24

Part II: Stories of Transitioning Toward Serving Doctoral Students 27

1. "A Joint Collaborative Task": The Africa International University
    Library (Nairobi) 27

2. "To Stretch the Imagination": The China Graduate School of Theology
    Library (Hong Kong).. 35

3. "Excellence Is a Journey": The South Asia Institute of Advanced
    Christian Studies Library (Bangalore)........................... 43

4. "A Missionary in and of Itself": The John Smyth Library of the
    International Baptist Theological Study Centre (Amsterdam) 52

5. What Do We See?: Some Reflections on the "Transition Stories" 58

Appendixes.. 65

    Appendix 1: Profile of Doctoral Candidates in the Majority World .. 67

    Appendix 2: Library Networks 73

For Further Reading 77

Contributors... 79

Foreword

Anyone involved in theological education globally recognizes that there are factors which continually demand that programs examine themselves and their future trajectories. These factors may take on various forms including difficult economics, technological challenges, unrest, and changing student demands, to name a few. Because of this, leaders in theological education often are looking for ways to better ground their educational offerings for the benefit of their students and constituents alike. Certainly, this applies to all sectors of theological education, including at the doctoral level and including the library.

Best Practice Guidelines for Theological Libraries Serving Doctoral Programs is a timely and appropriate resource that will help to steady libraries as pivotal contributors to the ongoing success of doctoral programs. While there are certainly influences which continue to challenge theological education leaders, this resource offers meaningful global insights, guidance, experience, and practical considerations to produce sound libraries. Particularly at the doctoral level, theological education leadership must ensure that considerable and pertinent resources are available for students to advance and achieve their educational objectives.

Through the global collaborative effort of eight contributing editors, all of whom have served doctoral students in the Majority World, *Best Practice Guidelines* provides the essentials to ensure that such libraries exist as an integral part of doctoral offerings. The editors have also developed this resource in such a way not only to challenge existing theological libraries, but also to help those who aspire to develop new doctoral programs. In order to inspire theological libraries to maximize their long-term effectiveness, the editors focus on five fundamental areas which embed sixteen leading principles within Part I of the book.

Libraries, unfortunately, are often a minimal component when planning doctoral programs. Within the first area, this book points out the critical need to not merely have librarians serve as caretakers of collections, but for the school to have a robust library development plan. Through practical and experienced considerations, especially for the Majority World settings, the editors extend much needed help on how to develop such a plan. As part of that planning, most schools will recognize that there is no library that could possibly offer its students every resource imaginable. Acknowledging this reality, the editors turn to a second important area when considering theological libraries, partnerships and collaboration, which are vital ways to maximize a library's resource capacity. Within this second area, *Best Practice Guidelines* provides real-life ways to explore relationships and tools to further enhance a theological library.

Once an institution has its pool of resources, the further development of that collection and its management are significant for any doctoral program's continued success. In this third area, the editors provide sound discernment which includes the nexus between the library collection and the curriculum, governing policies, a true focus on the unique needs of doctoral students within contexts, and their practical accessibility to the available resources.

The fourth area specifically addresses the roles of library personnel. The editors certainly do not see library personnel solely providing collateral support to doctoral programs, but rather they are serving in integral ways to reinforce the success of those programs. As such, this book encourages its readers to critically reflect on the potential contributions of library personnel as qualified library staff, creating a culture that is indeed student oriented, and focusing on professional development and support.

The final area addresses the information literacy of doctoral students. The editors make a good case for recognizing that not all doctoral level students have had the prior educational research experiences and training required to excel at the doctoral level. With this in mind, this fifth area provides vital practical measures to include in a curriculum, as well as ways to encourage students in an ongoing fashion. Appropriately, the editors further include the need for faculty input and suggest ways to engender a research culture within institutions.

Following their considerable recommendations based upon the five areas noted above, the editors go on to impart stories from their varied global contexts, relationships, and experiences. As they do so, the reader not only has the benefit of the practical guidelines already presented, but then in Part II of the book, many of those guidelines are illustrated through actual theological library scenarios. The editors do more than simply suggest guidelines, but rather have the credibility to suggest them based upon their own substantial experience in the field.

As mentioned earlier, theological education programs are regularly being challenged and those who lead them are constantly looking for ways to create stability within facets of their programs. *Best Practice Guidelines* offers institutional leaders immeasurable wisdom through global experiences to realize lasting, relevant, and contributing theological libraries that will enrich doctoral programs. Undoubtedly, as you read the pages in this book, the Lord will use them to help shape your theological libraries, which we trust will result in greater quality in theological education at the doctoral level for God's glory and the sake of his people.

Michael A. Ortiz, PhD
International Director, ICETE

Introduction

This book is the result of cooperation between librarians and faculty members from different continents. All of us are involved in serving doctoral students at theological schools in the Majority World (MW) and are intimately familiar with the joys and challenges of walking alongside these students on their research journeys. In many conversations, synchronous and asynchronous, we have shared ideas and our unique contextual experiences. These conversations have helped us shape and formulate recommendations for effective practices in theological libraries.

Even though we write as librarians, we hope that the issues raised also communicate with other stakeholders in theological schools. We are motivated by our common cause – to serve God and people through quality theological education – and we hope to highlight library-related aspects that might otherwise be overlooked. We firmly believe that libraries and librarians are indispensable contributors to student learning and need to be vital partners in research conversations.[1]

This book intends to raise awareness and stimulate discussion on the value and contribution of libraries to the success of doctoral programs in theological schools related to ICETE (International Council for Evangelical Theological Education). In this, it has several audiences in mind.

If you are an administrator, you will find an overview of:

- library-related issues that need to be contemplated and prepared before the start of a doctoral program;
- points to consider in the development of effective library personnel (roles, attitudes, professional training);
- ideas on the development of resources to support a research program (print, electronic, cooperative);
- activities and resources libraries should provide for the ongoing support of doctoral students.

---

1. A good library can contribute to a good reputation for the institution by manifesting the institution's academic values and research practices and even serve to attract students with academic competence and potential to pursue their doctoral qualification at the institution; cf. "The Value of Libraries for Research and Researchers," a RIN and RLUK report, March 2011; https://www.rluk.ac.uk/wp-content/uploads/2014/02/Value-of-Libraries-report.pdf (cited 7 May 2021).

If you are an accreditation officer charged with the evaluation of a doctoral program, you will find:

- an overview of library-related areas and aspects that need to be part of a self-study and the evaluation process during an accrediting visit;
- elements of what constitutes quality in theological libraries, as expressed through the cumulative experience and (realistic) best practices from theological librarians of different continents;
- general benchmarks related to holdings, personnel, cooperation, research, and information literacy training;
- ideas and recommendations to suggest to the institution under evaluation to guide their library development and assessment.

If you are a theological librarian in the Majority World, whose institution already has or plans to implement a doctoral program, you will find all of the above, as well as:

- names and ways to be in contact with librarians who serve in similar circumstances;
- areas and aspects upon which to reflect in self-assessment studies and in designing a library development plan;
- facets to consider in planning professional development for yourself and for your colleagues.

This book identifies five areas of intervention that need the attention of theological schools in the Majority World to optimize library operations to serve doctoral programs. Several principles in each of the five critical areas address aspects of best practice for theological librariesand serve as quality guidelines. The areas have each been written by a different contributor, then discussed and shaped in team conversations, resulting in the formulation of principles. An observant reader will notice style and emphasis differences, as well as repetitions. While the former are natural in such a composite work, the latter are intended and underline how each of the areas are fully interdependent with each other. Appendix 1, finally, summarizes information needs and research behaviors of doctoral students as observed and documented in the literature, which have guided us in our recommendations. Appendix 2 reinforces the need for cooperation in our interconnected world.

We have also included our experience. Librarians of four theological schools, who were part of the discussions, have shared their library's development process in transitioning to serve doctoral programs. We have tried to be as authentic and sincere as possible and not to succumb to the cultural trap of hiding problems behind a nice facade. As these stories come from different continents and contexts, we hope that other Majority World theological schools can glean lessons for themselves as they plan to start a doctoral program or go through an evaluation process of an already operating program.

The book relies on various sources (while not always quoting them explicitly), including the "Beirut Benchmarks"[2] for doctoral programs, standards of accrediting agencies (ICETE member organizations), and documents of various library organizations. A "Further Reading" list is provided at the back of the book.

The context of theological libraries is changing rapidly, and at the same time, there are also particular contextual distinctions. While we have attempted to develop best practice guidelines with input from different continents, these need to be incarnated to fit the situation in each local library and program. The implementation of each program might look different. Still, each theological library needs to contribute to the overarching goal of quality theological education and research in a way that can be verified. This is the library's mission and impact for God's kingdom.

---

2. The Beirut Benchmarks can be found at: https://icete.info/resources/the-beirut-benchmarks/.

Part I

Principles for Best Library Practice

Area 1: Integration of Library in Planning a Doctoral Program

Perhaps it is obvious that the library plays an indispensable role in any doctoral program. On the one hand, doctoral education is by its nature a self-directed learning endeavor. Students are expected to demonstrate initiative and engage in individual learning through scholarly research to complete a dissertation (or thesis). On the other hand, the host institution (whether a university, seminary, or other institution) is duty-bound to provide students with the necessary overall support, including a well-trained librarian and study facilities that are adequate, accessible, and fit for a doctoral program. The library is where doctoral candidates will naturally turn to gather information and resources for their research.

Principle #1: The library prominently participates in the preparation of the doctoral program

Sometimes institutions in the Majority World perceive the academic library to be a mere "keeper" of books and digital resources that plays the limited role of providing content to support the teaching undertaken by members of the faculty. Unfortunately, professional training for librarians is not considered essential by many institutions and so fails to find a place in the budget. It cannot be overstressed that the limited role of caretaker of a collection is insufficient if an academic library is to service a doctoral program.

a) **Plan for change in the library**: Because the information needs of doctoral students differ from undergraduates not only in quantity but in quality, the library needs to be part of the planning process from the inception of the doctoral program. This will help ensure the library can be sufficiently equipped with resources, facilities, and services before the program starts. A proactive and outward-looking approach needs to be taken by the library to fully and closely collaborate with other departments of the institution from the planning stage and throughout the institution's development and implementation of a doctoral program.[1] From the outset, the library liaison will (should) be included in considerations about areas of study and the number of programs to be offered at the doctoral level, the size of the student intake, their unique needs and strengths, and the budget to be allocated for study resources and facilities. Such awareness is particularly pertinent to situations in the Majority World, where many doctoral students – due to constraints in their living and family conditions – will require dedicated study space in the library for the purpose of their uninterrupted research and study.

b) **Create a library development plan**: A coherent library development plan will need to form part of the considerations before the initiation of a doctoral program. This will necessitate that the library must be bolstered with sufficient staff, facilities, and holdings to support the instructional objectives and learning outcomes of the new program.[2] The same fundamental role will also be reflected in the institutional budget, whether in terms of staff training, the expansion of research collections, space, and additional technological and research tools as well as other needs. The librarian must be fully informed and be a participant member of the conversation with the relevant doctoral program director and faculty in order to formulate plans outlining the necessary preparations. This will ensure that the theological school and library will provide students with the most relevant and useful research materials, facilities, and support. An evaluation of existing library resources, doctoral student needs, services available and necessary, and effective workflow options must precede and guide the library development plan. The library will report its activities at relevant departmental meetings so as to coordinate efforts and make the doctoral-program administration members aware of its level of preparedness, needs and challenges, and its availability and suitability for incoming doctoral students.

c) **Take initiative**: Sometimes the faculty and doctoral program director fail to involve the librarian in preparing and implementing the doctoral program. However, this should not stop the librarian from taking the initiative of telling others how library personnel can be of assistance and demonstrate its particular

---

1. The need for the library's involvement in program implementation will be discussed throughout the document.

2. Cf. ICETE, *Standards and Guidelines for Global Evangelical Theological Education.*

skills and creativity in serving students' information needs and supporting their dissertation projects. Especially in those institutions of the Majority World where a shortage of teaching faculty is commonplace, a well-prepared library can create new opportunities and demonstrate its value for enhancing the program by contributing its unique information skills to support student research in concert with the faculty and its departments.

Principle #2: The library prioritizes the unique needs of doctoral students and assigns personnel for the doctoral program

Doctoral journeys are unique – in their research topics as well as the processes – and so, besides an expansion of research collections, library services for doctoral students also need to be customized. The particular needs of doctoral students can be characterized as: knowledge of the literature and of research methodologies in their area, adequate time and resources, training in research and technology, and dialogue/conversation partners.[3] The following three aspects can help meet these needs.

a) **Companion**: Scholarship and research have often been characterized as conversation, and librarians, together with faculty, need to be part of conversations in which doctoral students engage. To walk with each individual doctoral student in his or her research and to cater to his or her specific and unique information needs is time-consuming and labor intensive. Such relationships often involve one-on-one contact and interviews to review an individual student's research habits and strategies and advise on improvements where necessary. The librarian works closely with the doctoral-program director (research director) and is involved in the orientation activities for doctoral students at the initiation of the program. As the go-to person for doctoral students and supervisors,[4] such library officers function as the "graduate students' librarian" (or whatever title the institution assigns to her/him). His or her responsibilities are not limited to collection development and management; instead, the librarian builds relationships with students and actively propagates available academic resources, information services, databases, research tools, and publication updates. The well-educated librarian

---

3. Appendix 1 spells out information needs and behaviors of doctoral students in more detail.

4. For more illustrations of the roles and functions of library personnel, please refer to Area 4 below.

will address topics particularly relevant to doctoral studies, such as academic writing, and they will help to create networks for contacts among students for sharing information and ideas. Librarians will also further academic dialogue and exchange among students and researchers. The librarian is open to consistently and creatively devising new roles to interact and support a student's research, whether through advice, counseling, answering enquiries, encouragement, personal demonstration, or innovative training.

b) **Guide**: The rapid appearance of new research materials and technological advancements and, thus, rapid changes in common research behaviors and procedures are confusing for students who return for doctoral studies after a break in their studies. The librarian strategically facilitates student use of new technologies by organizing training sessions and workshops. Usually this is time-consuming, hands-on, individualized training at the point of need. Since much of doctoral studies work is done under severe time pressure, the librarian needs to help students (and supervisors) become proficient with search technology and accessing resources. These needs imply that the librarian must continuously equip and develop himself or herself professionally and be well-acquainted with new resources and research skills to provide reliable guidance to students regarding the latest developments. Because of the scarcity of resources, librarians creatively develop ways to help students find these things vital to their work.

c) **Doctoral librarian**: Not all Majority World theological schools will find it possible to hire additional library personnel when planning the launch of a doctoral program. However, it should undoubtedly be an essential consideration when drawing up the budget for the program. Sometimes it will be possible to entrust an already employed librarian with the responsibility of providing services to doctoral students and to assist in the development of this person to meet the new program's unique needs. Such an individual should be appointed during the planning stage for the doctoral program so that a strategic approach to overall library support for doctoral students and their supervisors can be established by the academic and library leadership in consultation with each other.

The services of a special librarian will increase the likelihood of success for a doctoral program. Such a special librarian will be available either face-to-face or electronically to guide students through the matrix of various resources, research tools, and technologies found in the library and on the internet. Preferably this individual will have professional training, whether through formal education or on-the-job experience, and will have a firm grasp of both research needs and the challenges and uncertainties commonly found among doctoral students.

Area 2: Partnerships and Collaboration

The excellence of doctoral-level education depends to a considerable degree on the quality and efficiency of library services and the availability of relevant academic resources. However, no theological library, let alone libraries in Majority World theological schools, can claim to be sufficiently equipped to service all the specialized research needs of doctoral students and faculty members. They cannot function in isolation. For this reason, libraries are dependent not only on strategic and reliable collaboration within the institution, but also on partnerships outside of the organization. As mentioned above, libraries collaborate with faculty, supervisors, and program administrators within the institution for mutual benefit. They also actively establish partnerships with other academic and theological libraries locally and internationally. While research students' information needs in the current digital era are more complex, dynamic, and ever-changing, the possibilities for cooperation have also advanced.

Principle #3: The library collaborates with faculty in research-related areas

Faculty members play an essential role in library development for doctoral services. The contribution of faculty members who have an in-depth knowledge of their fields can empower the library in the quality of acquisitions, in developing research skills, and with enhancing the library's services by their recommendations. The following areas hold promising potential for the library to develop partnerships with faculty.

a) **Curriculum development**: As explained in the principles for Area #1, a librarian should be part of the curriculum development team and remain abreast of all curricular decisions. Such engagement helps the librarian to evaluate the relevance and sufficiency of existing resources for supporting the curriculum and to improve library holdings as a response to new initiatives and upcoming programs. Librarians bring additional knowledge on the availability and accessibility of resources, prepare estimates for adequate funding, and contribute suggestions for constantly improving services.

b) **Collection development**: Faculty members are not only consumers of information but also information creators and networkers. The knowledge and support of faculty members help the library to develop useful and relevant research resources. In particular, doctoral programs will need specific input from faculty as to adequate print and electronic resources related to this additional curriculum. The head and faculty of each department, as well as the research director (doctoral-program coordinator), shall be responsible for a regular evaluation of their department's available library resources, for offering recommendations for new acquisitions, and for the removal of resources whose value has diminished.

c) **Research skills development** (user education and information literacy): The more comfortable doctoral students feel about their research and library skills, the more efficiently they will engage in the use of library resources and services. The library's user-education program should be designed in consultation and cooperation with supervisors and faculty members involved in the doctoral program. This kind of ongoing cooperation will leverage the faculty's knowledge and skills, and faculty will, on their side, enhance the awareness among students that the library is their ally. Faculty members are great marketing agencies for library services and collections. During training sessions and workshops, faculty members can offer insights on the quality of library resources in each department, suggest methods of effective search and utilization of information, and guide doctoral students to subject-specific resources beyond the local library. In consultation with faculty, specialized training sessions can be created for each department and course. Such collaboration efforts are mutually beneficial for the librarian and faculty members.[5]

d) **Coordination of research visits**: Supervisors and faculty members are subject specialists who can provide guidance for arranging research visits by doctoral students to other libraries that are possibly better resourced in a specific research area. Through their networks, faculty are also equipped to connect students with external specialists on their topic. Librarians are frequently members of different networks and can leverage their personal and professional relationships with peers in other institutions to the same effect. A mutual effort by librarians and faculty to plan and arrange a study visit by the

---

5. See more on this in Principle #15.

student to another institution's library will contribute much to such research endeavors' efficiency and success.

Principle #4: The library collaborates with other libraries locally and internationally

a) **Inter-Library Loan (ILL)**: No library is completely funded or resourced for specialized doctoral studies. In the Majority World context, theological libraries are confronted with the challenge of meeting the research-information needs of its clientele in a context of meagre budgets. To overcome the scarcity of research resources and for maximal stewardship of available financial resources, theological libraries that serve doctoral students must collaborate with other libraries via networking, Inter-Library Loan (ILL), and other resource-sharing agreements.

A handful of existing models are worthy of emulation. A theological library can join efforts with other theological libraries in the region to form a cooperative network for mutual benefit. The Joint Library Committee (JLC) in Bangalore, India,[6] is a collaborative model that is more than thirty years old, and among theological libraries, it is one of the most successful in the Majority World. At present, eighteen theological libraries in Bangalore are members of JLC. Users affiliated with member libraries can borrow books and journal articles from other libraries. JLC has a union catalogue with over 200,000 bibliographic records. Students and faculty can borrow books, journal articles, and theses via Inter-Library Loan (ILL) for a specific period.

An ILL agreement with state, university, or other libraries helps libraries invest their funds sensibly and benefit from borrowing (rather than purchasing) expensive books or journals. Theological libraries can focus on developing their core collections and obtain rarely needed resources from other libraries. Clearly stated ILL guidelines among libraries, consideration of legal restrictions, and the allocation of necessary finances in the budget to pay for ILL services, advance the viability of such networks. Borrowing libraries are fully responsible for the safe return of books and agree to pay replacement costs in case of loss or damage.

b) **Document Delivery Service (DDS)**: The internet has revolutionized how information is acquired and delivered. Sharing of resources becomes easier to the degree that libraries are connected to the internet. Document-delivery agreements can be designed with theological libraries internationally

---

6. http://jlcbangalore.in.

for the acquisition of book chapters and journal articles. The institution's administration, the doctoral-program director, a faculty member, or a supervisor might need to initiate the first contact between the Majority World and the international library to negotiate an agreement.

Member libraries of such document delivery networks adopt various Information and Communications Technology (ICT) solutions to share articles, chapters from books, and other materials among its network. A good internet connection and a scanner play a critical role (often mobile phone apps are also used). Additionally, a designated email ID will help keep track of user requests and fulfilments. It is recommended that patrons do not approach other libraries directly for fulfilling their requests but always channel the request through a librarian. A personalized email note with a scanned copy of the article will then be emailed to the requesting library and finally to the doctoral student.

When sharing copyrighted materials, the librarian must ensure that ownership and licensing rights are respected and no infringement occurs. This is important in international contexts as different countries have different copyright restrictions. It is always advisable to lace a copyright declaration page at the end of each scanned copy of an article or chapter to alert users that the materials are for personal and educational use only. Each member library will need to orient their patrons on copyright matters and ensure that copyrighted materials are not indiscriminately shared or posted on public sites.

Area 3: Collection Development and Management

A library is more than a storehouse for books. According to the *Cambridge Dictionary*, a library is "a building, room or organization with a collection, especially of books, for people to read or borrow, usually without payment." In this area, we are concerned with both aspects of the definition of a library: (1) use and accessibility of the books, and (2) the nature of the collection and how best to manage it. These two issues will be addressed in terms of several principles that explain how best to serve doctoral students through the library collection and its use.

Principle #5: The library's collection serves the curriculum, including the doctoral program

A library collection exists to directly support a theological school's curriculum; the doctoral program is no exception. This means that a theological school cannot start a doctoral program without having prepared a suitable research collection. Even though there might be cooperative agreements with other libraries for ILL or DDS, a school cannot solely rely on those holdings to cover information needs for the new program. As a learning resource, the collection's focus should be adequate and specific to the courses being taught and topics being researched. This means that new courses or programs will require a substantial financial investment into the library to bring the specific areas defined by the new programs to the required level. Curriculum changes without an investment in library resources damage the course program as well as the library's quality of learning support. The curriculum and library should be an integrated whole. A well-designed collection development policy will clarify this to the school's leadership.

Principle #6: Collection development and management are governed by policy

a) **Justification**: Every library should have a collection development policy written by the library staff and discussed with and endorsed by the faculty and the theological school's leadership. By making library holdings more visible to faculty and allowing the school's leadership to understand how the library operates, this document governs acquisition decisions. It provides an argument for the (financial) needs of the library in the context of the curriculum. The presence of such a document will make the library a conversation partner in discussions that touch on the planning and implementation of a doctoral program in the institution.

b) **Contents of the policy**: It is advisable to set up a collection development policy according to the guidelines that have been developed for this purpose by the International Federation of Library Associations (IFLA) Section on Acquisition and Collection Development, available online in English, French, Italian, Russian, Spanish, and Arabic.[7] The document explains the intricacies of drafting a collection development policy and illuminates the nature of a library collection.

The policy should include a library mission statement, a brief statement about the intended users, a description of the educational program(s) being served, a description of the collection as it is, and how the library acquisition's budget will accommodate and reinforce the various types of resources. In

---

7. See IFLA, "Guidelines for a Collection Development Policy Using the Conspectus Model," https://www.ifla.org/files/assets/acquisition-collection-development/publications/gcdp-en.pdf.

addition, there should be a plan for the development of the collection: what kinds of resources, in which languages, in what format, limitations in subjects, special disciplines, or areas of attention. The collection development policy also includes a section on how to deal with donations (gifts policy) and describes the process and criteria for evaluating materials to be discarded (weeding policy). The policy should have a timetable for when to review and possibly revise it. The IFLA document also contains various measuring tools to define the current scope of the collection.

Principle #7: The collection development policy emphasizes acquisition for the doctoral program

A collection development policy identifies areas of interest for the local theological library. It is essential that some space in the policy be dedicated to the needs of doctoral students. They will require different resources than undergraduate and graduate students (e.g. handbooks on research methods and specialized monographs). These needs should be outlined and defined in the collection development policy and will result in financial provisions for special acquisitions related to doctoral programs. The collection development policy may be shared with potential donors to include them in developing adequate library holdings.

It is good practice to set aside a certain percentage of the acquisition budget for doctoral students' purchase requests. Of course, not everything can be acquired. Still, by purchasing books needed for individuals research needs, the library gathers information regarding repeating needs, new or important releases in specific research areas, and titles not available through ILL. Having dedicated funds set apart for precisely these needs makes life easier for doctoral students and supervisors. For example, the amount dedicated to acquisitions for doctoral students could be a certain percentage of the budget or a fixed amount that would equal the costs of one (or more) book(s) per doctoral student per year.

Principle #8: The library provides access to print and electronic resources

a) **Balancing print and electronic resources**: The collection development policy will state the library's approach to acquiring and handling print and electronic resources. The standard library model is still to have an extensive print collection with limited electronic resources. This creates problems for many Majority World theological schools when they attempt to serve doctoral programs. While it is imperative to develop a substantial print collection of indispensable works, electronic access to relevant resources will be vital during doctoral studies. Therefore ways need to be explored to acquire access to electronic resources. As research students often study at a geographical distance from the school, the physical collection is often of limited value to them. Accordingly they prefer remotely available full-text electronic resources for ease of access.

b) **Accessibility issues**: Libraries in the Majority World find themselves in different circumstances regarding technological infrastructure and guaranteed access to electronic resources. Some contexts will not have reliable electricity or sufficient internet bandwidth. A theological school and library will need to find creative solutions: reliable and continuous access to electricity, good WiFi capabilities, copying and scanning possibilities, computer stations (even though the trend moves inexorably toward the use of mobile phones and tablets for access), and flash drives with resources/readers (in the framework of existing copyright regulations).

c) **Purchase of e-collections or creation of one's own e-collections**: In most cases, it will be financially and legally impossible for a Majority World school to set up its own electronic collection which will be sufficient for doctoral studies. A limited electronic collection (created in the framework of existing copyright regulations) might still be feasible. To ensure extended and effective use, the creation of such a collection needs to be well planned and implemented using the latest technology.

There are various collections of ebooks and e-journals available for purchase or licensing, but they are quite costly. In case a library decides to purchase electronic resources, it may prioritize investment in relevant ebooks hoping that access to journal articles might become possible through ILL and document delivery agreements.

d) **Cooperation with existing ventures**: When financial resources are available, it is wise to seek out cooperative initiatives with like-minded institutions to establish a joint online library. An excellent example of this is the Theological Libraries Ebook Lending Project.[8] Another possibility is the Digital Theological Library,[9] with its very affordable option for the Majority World theological

---

8. ATLA's E-book Lending Program: https://www.theologicalebooks.org/opac/#index.
9. DTL, http://www.digitaltheologicallibrary.org.

schools of the Global Digital Theological Library.[10] These can also serve as a model of what could be set up in one's own context.

However, there are other realistic options for provision of electronic access to resources. Lack of funding shouldn't be an unsurpassable obstacle:

1) Open access resources: Students are encouraged to create an account at the Open Access Digital Theological Library.[11] This resource is sponsored by an international group of theological schools and made available free of charge to theology students worldwide. At the time of writing, it already includes over 200,000 ebooks. As open access publishing will develop further, the OADTL will continue to catalogue high-quality new content. Also, other resources are available, like the Directory of Open Access Journals.[12] There are many other open access collections available online. A particularly useful one can be found on the website of Duke University Libraries.[13] There are also various collections of open access dissertations available.[14] The library must create a website page, or have a presence in the school's learning management system (Moodle, Blackboard, etc.), where links to all these resources are made available to students.

2) International contacts: The librarian needs to have good working relationships with librarians from related, possibly international, institutions with reliable electronic access. This will make it easy to facilitate (formal and informal) ILL and document deliveries. Most libraries are willing and able to provide scans of articles or chapters from books for doctoral students. The library must engage all options that allow doctoral students to participate in the global academic discourse.

3) Research visits to other libraries: Even before implementing a doctoral program, it is helpful to identify good research collections nearby to have recourse to them when necessary and encourage doctoral students to spend research time in these libraries. Students may also need to spend weeks abroad at a like-minded institution with extensive print and electronic collections. It may be possible

---

10. Global Digital Theological Library, https://globaldtl.org.

11. OADTL, https://oadtl.org.

12. DOAJ, https://doaj.org.

13. Duke University Libraries, https://guides.library.duke.edu/openreligion/.

14. http://www.opendissertations.org; http://www.oatd.org; and http://www.dart-europe.eu.

to collaborate with the host school's leadership or funding partners to set up a bursary fund for travel to and accommodation at these research libraries.

Principle #9: The library fosters accessibility and sharing through a recognized classification system and online catalogue

A room full of books is useful only when there is a way to find a needed volume. For this reason, it is essential to use an internationally recognized classification system. Some countries will have a national (or regional) classification system in place. If this is not the case, or if the national classification is considered inadequate for any reason, there are two widely accepted international options: Library of Congress Classification (LCC) and Dewey Decimal Classification (DDC). Classification assistance (mostly for English language resources) is readily available at Classify.[15] The use of a widely accepted classification system enables the library to save cataloging time by downloading bibliographic records and also prepares students for efficient searching during their international research trips to libraries that use the same or a similar system.

Most professional Library Management Systems (LMS) offer a publicly accessible online catalog. Often they are also compatible with mobile technologies. Mobile access is indispensable if a theological school has students studying at a distance. An online catalog populated with catalogued print and electronic resources makes it easy for users to find in a "one-stop-search" resources available in the library or to access electronic resources remotely. License fees for most commercial LMS packages are prohibitive, so in many cases, it is necessary to make use of open-source alternatives like Koha or Evergreen.[16] Open-source solutions can be downloaded and used free of charge but often require dedicated IT support staff. While librarians can become proficient in operating such LMS, installation and maintenance sometimes fall outside of the usual scope of the skills of librarians.

---

15. See Classify, http://classify.oclc.org/classify2. Extensive LCC documentation is available here: https://www.loc.gov/aba/cataloging/classification/. For DDC, it is advisable to use the four-volume handbook: http://www.worldcat.org/oclc/907324722 or the single volume abridged version: http://www.worldcat.org/oclc/1089910521. Online DDC documentation is available at WebDewey (https://www.oclc.org/en/dewey/webdewey.html), but subscription costs might be prohibitive (and owning the print handbook will do away with any pressing need for this).

16. Koha (http://www.koha.org); Evergreen (http://www.evergreen-ils.org).

Area 4: The Role(s) of Library Personnel

As mentioned in Area #1, the library is an integral part of an educational institution and needs to be fully involved in developing and implementing doctoral programs. Quite possibly, this will also include a review and/or reevaluation of its role. Faculty often seem to perceive the role of a theological library merely as a support to teaching and learning,[17] but this definition is not enough for serving doctoral programs. Matters are more complex, and libraries can and should play multiple and varied roles in the educational process at all levels. Besides providing access to print and digital resources and physical study space, librarians facilitate research activities, offer reference services, educate through information literacy classes, and consult in many other areas related to research and publication. The ability to offer these services, however, directly depends on the number and education of library staff and on the vision that the institution and library staff have for the role of the librarian.

Principle #10: The institution has sufficient qualified library staff

Theological schools in the Majority World find themselves in very different realities when it comes to the number and education of library staff. Some will have one or more trained librarians; at other institutions, librarians will need to develop necessary skills "on the go." An institution that plans or operates doctoral studies will need to make a conscious and concerted effort to ensure that the library is sufficiently equipped for a doctoral program not only in the area of resources but also in securing qualified personnel.[18]

In terms of skills and training, the lead librarian will preferably have both a theology and a library degree, have a good knowledge of theological literature, and be savvy in the field of technology. While this might not yet be the case when the school starts planning for a doctoral program, it is essential that the librarian actively develops knowledge and skills in each of these areas. Besides professional qualities, a library staff needs to have a mature spirituality and effective communication and problem-solving abilities. They engage with various campus groups, such as faculty, IT personnel, doctoral

---

17. The 2017 Ithaka S+R research report (Cooper and Schonfeld, "Supporting the Changing Research Practices of Religious Studies Scholars," 41), points out that faculty often mistakenly believe the library is influential for undergraduate students and for teaching activities only, but does not play a role in research, nor is it relevant for doctoral students' needs.

18. There will definitely be differences depending on the context as to how "sufficient" and "qualified" is defined. The school will necessarily heed practices and regulations of the country where it is located.

students, and external researchers. They must be able to take initiative, have a depth of "common sense," work independently and collaboratively, and prove themselves flexible and creative in adapting to various situations. Some of these qualities are spelled out in greater depth below.[19]

Principle #11: Library staff consistently emphasize a "service culture" and continuously improve their user-orientation

a) **Service-centered approach**: It may seem redundant to emphasize the need for a service-centered approach in a library, which, by definition, is a service institution. But, given the many pressures and expectations that librarians in theological schools in the Majority World face – for example, lack of personnel and finances, isolation and few possibilities for professional development, extremely fast technological developments which need to be mastered to stay on top of things – there is sometimes the temptation to cocoon oneself from the outer world and just try to get the job done. It is important to regularly remind oneself of the attitude and approach that is part of a librarian's calling and profession; namely, leaving behind a clerk/administrative attitude and perspective and focusing on the individual and his or her information needs. Library and academic leadership should promote a balance between goal-orientation and people-orientation and create an environment in which both attitudes are encouraged.

b) **User-oriented approach**: Librarians have been described as door-openers and connectors. Their service includes connecting: (1) people (doctoral students) and resources (in all formats and places), (2) people to people (doctoral students with relevant scholars, conferences, and other learning/scholarship communities), and (3) people and technology (knowing and promoting technologies potentially useful for doctoral students in their research process). To manage all these services means the librarian must understand the needs, cultural backgrounds, and research habits of doctoral students using the library while keeping eyes and ears open to available and accessible print and digital resources and technologies as well as scholarship venues and communities. The library is well-rooted locally and contextually – this is

---

19. See also Jim Dunkley's characterization of a theological librarian who "must have a sense of theology as a whole, a sense of the church, a sense of the community of scholarship, and a sense of care for people" (Dunkley, 230–31). There will be a considerable variation in mode and degree of involvement in these areas – because of personality and job differences – but a clear dedication to all four areas is vital.

reflected in collection development, in offered services, and in communication patterns – while at the same time open to global developments.

Ideally librarians, sometimes more than institutional supervisors, become catalysts in the research process. They are networkers who have embraced a need-oriented approach and who notice gaps and fill them with their unique set of skills. The library functions a bit like a "hub" for meeting and connecting as the library plans and/or contributes to various activities that enable a community of learning and exchange of research findings. For these reasons, the library needs to focus itself outward rather than inward, with library staff who are well-connected to relevant offices in one's own institution as well as networked across a range of international contacts for ILL and resource exchange.

Principle #12: Library staff are continuously involved in life-long learning and professional development

a) **Academic status**: Theological libraries in the Majority World find themselves in very different situations in terms of number and professional education of staff. While there is an "ideal" theological librarian who has degrees in theology, library, and technology, in reality, this aspiration is challenging to achieve. A professionally trained librarian's benefits are obvious, especially if the educational and research-catalyst role of a librarian is acknowledged. The institution is well advised to strive for this goal and for the outcomes that flow from it.

Librarians with tailored educational preparation and research capacity fully deserve an academic status on par with faculty. Such academic standing makes them colleagues with teaching staff and enables engagement in all relevant functions, including teaching suitable courses, especially those related to research.

b) **Life-long learning**: We have emphasized the need for continuous development of each library staff member. They are confronted with rapid and profound technological changes, together with changes in publishing modes and various electronic-resource business models and developments in educational formats that have an effect on the library. It is therefore critical that they remain abreast of new developments. All library staff members must be involved in professional exchange with peers, and so participation at local and international librarians' conferences and in library associations needs to be encouraged. Library schools in the Majority World are slow in developing online courses in librarianship and/or adapting their longstanding curricula to the technological developments and the changed philosophy of library services. But where distance and online librarianship education is available, such courses can help gain professional librarianship training "on the job."

c) **Local and international exchange**: Cooperation and exchange between librarians in theological libraries in the Majority World who support doctoral programs will also enrich professional development. Often librarians in other institutions have confronted similar challenges and pressures and have developed creative solutions to better fulfill their calling. Such innovations can be adapted to fit other contexts. The expertise of staff can be disseminated via staff-exchange programs. Majority World libraries often face a shortage of trained staff. Staff exchange offers an opportunity for needy libraries to access the help of trained librarians from other institutions. Such a dynamic of professional exchange can be arranged on a mutual understanding between institutions.

Professional mentors, to whom Majority World librarians can relate, are a particular source of encouragement and growth. Such people embrace librarianship as a ministry and are ready to serve others in the interest of advancing thriving theological education in other countries. They are often keen to travel to a location or consult from a distance to work alongside individuals appointed to work as librarians. Their input customarily straddles the line between training and mentorship.

Area 5: Information Literacy in Doctoral Program(s)

Definition: Information Literacy can be defined as a set of skills and competencies to locate, evaluate, and use information ethically and effectively. It is closely related to computer and library skills, research skills, and critical thinking; that is, it combines hands-on skills and thinking abilities and habits.

There seems to be a general assumption that students at the doctoral level, having undergone library instruction at preceding levels, are already conversant with finding and using information resources available in any library and on the internet. Additionally, it is often assumed that such students have developed adequate research and technology skills. However, the reality for many theology doctoral students in the Majority World is that they enroll in doctoral studies long after completing a master's program. Research practices and habits will have changed considerably in the interim due to rapid advances both in technology and the availability of electronic resources. Most doctoral students enroll in a different institution from the one where they did their master's training (often in a foreign country) and so are unfamiliar with new library environments.

Information and research literacy are critical components for equipping students with approaches and skills to be effective searchers, evaluators, and information users. They are also essential tools for lifelong learning. While most higher learning institutions have elaborate training programs for undergraduates and a few more at the master's level, few focus on PhD level students.

Principle #13: The library develops an Information Literacy policy and curriculum

a) **Information Literacy policy**: Every library should have a comprehensive Information Literacy (IL) policy developed by the library, discussed with the faculty, and approved by the respective administrative organs. This document guides the library's focus on doctoral student research skills and needs. It allows the school's leadership to appreciate the role the library plays in equipping doctoral students. This is the area where librarians work most closely together with subject area faculty. The IL policy runs in tandem with the institution's academic research and writing policies and practices to provide synergy with other arms of the institution. It should state the audience and scope it targets, include a statement of purpose, goals, and objectives, outline the pedagogical underpinnings for the program, the role of various stakeholders, and expected benefits from the program. Such a document usually covers Information Literacy for all library users and includes a special section regarding doctoral students.

b) **Information Literacy curriculum**: Before deciding on a curriculum or framework for IL interventions for doctoral students, the library will need to be very clear about the skills and competencies these users have at entry (a survey might help), how they approach their studies and research, and what program learning outcomes are expected from students. When librarians understand the stages of a research process, they can decide which niches are filled by the faculty, which the library can fill, and how to do this most efficiently and effectively. The curriculum will consist of several components that focus on different competencies, use different pedagogies, and are mutually complementary:

    1)   orientation and training for doctoral students, in several successive phases, offered at the beginning of studies and continuously building

upon each other throughout the doctoral process. These can be workshops, hands-on-seminars, units in existing (research methods) courses, and/or a stand-alone information literacy/competency course.

2) training for senior researchers and supervisors (who are "first contact" persons for doctoral students) that refreshes their skills and enables them to offer training to research students at the point of need.

3) development of supporting "self-help tools" that are available at the point of need after hours without the presence of librarian or supervisor, for example, online tutorials for various aspects of information search, evaluation, and use as well as for available databases and services.

Principle #14: The library provides initial and ongoing orientation for doctoral students

a) **Initial orientation**: Together with the general orientation for doctoral students entering the program, school administrators should allocate space and time for the librarian to conduct special sessions related to research and information skills. Doctoral students need to be introduced to library resources and services focused specifically upon their unique needs as advanced researchers. There should be initial training to locate materials in their field(s) of study in all formats, on the use of catalog and various databases, an overview of research tools and materials available worldwide, a strategy for assessing the quality, reliability, and relevance of found resources, and a presentation of services that the local library offers research and distance students. It is important that students enjoy a positive experience with library-related aspects at the beginning of the process and are encouraged to return subsequently with individual questions. The initial orientation should conclude with students empowered to connect with a library subject specialist, supervisor/faculty member in their subject area, or a contact person who will assist them in their areas of research.

b) **Ongoing orientation**: The induction of doctoral students must present the library as the place where the student can expect to find answers to their information needs throughout the course of their doctoral study. The ongoing reference help and training focuses on individualized and customized support and depends on the skills of the student, the research stage, and the student's location and situation. The librarian must develop an empathetic understanding of students' research topics and through various reference services (face-to-face, online chats, e-mail) function as an additional conversation partner for the doctoral researcher. The primary conversation partner for the doctoral student in his or her research is the supervisor and other relevant faculty members. However, when supervision has been assigned to adjunct faculty or a visiting specialist, or if supervisors are too busy with teaching and their own research activities, doctoral students can sometimes find themselves left alone and isolated. Sporadic conversations with a subject librarian who knows the literature, who can ask the right questions, and can point to certain names, ideas, and resources will prove invaluable and help sustain the doctoral student through the tiring journey.

At later stages, students may need support in areas such as dealing with copyright issues (permissions to include material of other authors, asserting copyright for their own materials), reference management software, and publication processes.

Principle #15: Librarians collaborate with faculty in Information Literacy interventions

As the Information Literacy Policy and Curriculum will have laid out, library and faculty collaborate in creating a conducive research environment for doctoral students, individually and through doctoral program structures. Because Information and Research Literacy is best taught not as a one-time activity but as a continuous process embedded in various units, librarian-faculty collaboration becomes critical. The distinct but complementary roles of librarians and faculty occasion opportunities where the two come together to determine how they can best leverage each other's skills for success. Such interactions will include librarians and faculty having conversations that lead to a shared understanding of what Information Literacy is and its benefits to students. The result should be the embedding of IL components in some units. At the same time, librarians also engage in one-time presentations to doctoral students on specific IL topics, either as part of a taught unit or as a stand-alone presentation.

Principle #16: The library is part of the institution's research culture

This principle is related to the changing role of a theological library when doctoral studies are added. That is to say, the library not only supports others in their learning and research activities but also upholds the value of life-long learning for librarians themselves. Librarians are proactive information specialists familiar with the research process and information needs arising at its different stages. Library staff themselves are involved in or have done research, so they have experienced problems and roadblocks in the research process and therefore understand its joys and challenges. Familiarity with untangling research problems for themselves enables a librarian to empathize with students and to help them understand information needs that change throughout the research process, information-seeking and utilization practices, what resources users typically find or fail to locate (locally, on the internet, or through acquaintances), and why these dynamics occur. Librarians are well placed to think creatively and suggest workarounds when students face problems. By being engaged in their own research projects,[20] librarians can contribute to and promote a research culture among students and faculty at the institution, support the ongoing discussion around research, and nourish a community of research and learning as well as the exchange of research findings.

---

20. Librarians are often encouraged to engage in research conversations by writing book reviews. This supports their collection development, enables them to provide reference advice, contributes to their professional development, and benefits the academic community.

Part II

Stories of Transitioning Toward Serving Doctoral Students

1. "A Joint Collaborative Task": The Africa International University Library (Nairobi)

Dr. Ephraim Mudave, University Librarian

Africa International University (AIU) was started as Nairobi Evangelical Graduate School of Theology (NEGST) in 1983 by the Association of Evangelicals in Africa (AEA). The goal was to provide training for pastors beyond the basic certificate and diploma levels. The initiative was informed by the observed crisis of "Christo-paganism" in African Christianity intensified by a lack of African biblical theologians with advanced training to provide leadership in combating this trend. The government of Kenya awarded AIU a university charter in March 2011. It has since continued to develop undergraduate and graduate programs, particularly in business, IT, development studies, and counselling/psychology, in addition to theology.

AIU is committed to offering education with a passion for

- God, God's word, and God's world,
- truth, integrity, service,
- excellence, justice, beauty, life, and creation.

To this end, there are four schools: NEGST (School of Theology); School of Business and Economics; School of Education, Arts and Social Sciences; and Institute for the Study of African Realities.

Discussions on adding doctoral programs at the institution began years ago but took shape around 2002. The librarian was involved when it became clear that the envisioned date for the commencement of doctoral programs would be 2005. Those three years were committed to planning, fund-raising, and facility upgrading. At that time, programs included MA Theology, MA Missions, MA Biblical Studies, MA Translation Studies, and an MDiv program. There was a Certificate and Diploma in Christian Ministries focused on equipping women (mostly spouses of students) for effective ministry. Proposed programs were a PhD in Biblical Studies and a PhD in Translation Studies. The purpose of these two programs was to train researchers at the highest academic level so they would provide a valuable contribution to Bible scholarship in Africa and the world and offer translation consulting and training.

Image 1: Africa International University Library

At the end of 2002, the library had about 31,000 titles, including 2,500 bound journal volumes. Almost all library operations were manual and in need of automation. The library was headed by a librarian with a master's in Library Science who was aided by two professional staff with bachelor's training and three persons not trained in library science but with experience of working in the library. I was the deputy librarian then and so was able to follow all steps of the process. At that time, I had a bachelor's degree in library science. Later I received a master's degree and, finally, doctoral training in information studies. We clearly realized the need to train existing staff to serve doctoral students. The visit by two librarians from the US in mid-2004 further aided the library's preparation process since they had experience working in institutions that offered doctoral programs and in data conversion. Visiting scholars the same year who consulted on the development of the programs also had useful input for the library's development.

The institution had a library committee chaired by a faculty member on behalf of the academic dean, with the librarian as secretary. The committee incorporated two representatives from the student council, one representative from the Information and Communications Technology (ICT) department, and two faculty members, making a total of seven members, all with voting rights. The plan to develop the library to support doctoral programs was shared in the committee, and a Library Development Project was birthed. Since the library committee chair was the head of the Translation and Linguistics department, the committee had firsthand information on the progress of the development of the doctoral program. The librarian's involvement from the initial discussions gave the library a picture of the direction of the development.

The Library Development Project had five focus areas, namely: periodicals, books, space, technology, and budget/staff.

Periodicals

Periodicals provide up-to-date research information in the field. Efforts to expand the journal collection for both biblical and translation studies saw the number of journal titles rise from about 150 to 230. Expansion meant a renewal of subscriptions that had lapsed. The staff received relevant title recommendations for subscriptions from concerned departments through the doctoral studies coordinator. The staff identified key journal titles and subscribed to them. Those with broken runs were listed for the acquisition of missing issues. We subscribed to relevant databases, such as ATLAS, EBSCOHost, ATLA RDB, and JSTOR.

Books

After a collection evaluation, the need to expand the reference and general research section became obvious. Specific leading commentaries and reference titles were to be purchased. Collaboration with faculty from the concerned departments included quarterly reports from the library to the doctoral development committee on resources ordered and received, and the financial statements of both orders and receipts. There were two lecturers from biblical and translation studies who collected paper catalogues, accessed online catalogs, and presented order lists to the librarian who ensured that the resources were acquired and delivered. There was no collection development policy, so whatever lecturers in the two pioneering doctoral departments proposed was adopted.

Image 2: Students at AIU Library

Several books were out of print, especially for biblical studies. Among the leading publishers heavily used were Mohr-Siebeck, Brill, Eisenbrauns, Society for Biblical Literature, IVP, Walter De Gruyter, Continuum, John Wiley, Langham Literature, Routledge, and Fortress Press. We had to search online bookstores and archives for seminal out-of-print and used titles. Leading was Dove Booksellers, who provided most of these out-of-print titles. The Theological Book Network (TBN) was very instrumental in collection development by negotiating better prices with leading publishers in the US and in collating orders and shipping. At this point, we hired one permanent staff member to take charge of orders and processing.

Like the Theological Book Network and Langham, the partnerships and collaborations with individuals and institutions played an important role in collection development. The excellent working relationship between the library and faculty was an added advantage because the subject specialists felt in charge while the library staff felt adequately supported by faculty to discharge their duties. We benefited from the faculty's subject knowledge of useful resources for doctoral programs.

Space

It is a common practice that resident doctoral students require dedicated study space in the library. We did not have a problem with space since our institution had a small population of about 250–300 students registered each semester. Part of the library building on the first floor had, until that time, been used for office space. We had to construct a staircase to access the floor from the library. Half of the area upstairs was converted into doctoral study carrels, the rest set apart for bound and back issues of journals. The doctoral carrels were to accommodate at least twelve students for a start. The increased acquisition of books also required more shelf space. Several rows of shelves were procured, and since we had just moved to the new library building a few years earlier, there was space on the ground floor to accommodate these.

Technology

As mentioned, we needed to automate library processes, so the library committee undertook the search for an appropriate library management system. The library presented a list of specific functions expected of the new system, and several software packages were reviewed in light of these functions. The IT manager was incorporated into the library committee at this stage to ensure that we acquired a system that was compatible with the rest of the institutional ICT infrastructure. It took five months to settle on a suitable system and have Alice Graduate installed. At that point, a librarian trained in ICT was hired and trained on the new software. Much later, we migrated from Alice Graduate to the open-source software Koha with the help of the IT department staff. This collaboration created a strong partnership between the library and the IT department that we have continued to enjoy over the years. The system librarian is the link staff between the two departments.

Moving the library catalog online meant that library users required access to computers for searching. We started with only four computers dedicated specifically for access to the Online Public Access Catalog (OPAC). However, gradually a multimedia center was developed within the library with eighteen computers to access online resources. For doctoral students, the scholarship that each received included a new laptop. In addition to computers, the library purchased several hand-held scanners to aid the new automated operations.

The doctoral carrels were each connected to the university's network; later, wireless internet access was provided. A printer was installed in the PhD room to ease printing for students. A state-of-the-art photocopier was bought to which students could send their work. A flatbed scanner was also procured for those who preferred scanning documents over photocopying.

Conversion of the Card Catalog

The installation of the new library management system in May 2004 saw the beginning of a retrospective catalogue conversion exercise. We had more than 29,000 records for books that needed reclassification from Dewey Decimal to Library of Congress Classification (as required by the accrediting body, see below). We also had to convert the records from the manual card catalog. About 9,600 of the records were in a program called Librarian's Helper. With the help of a visiting librarian, we managed to convert them into MARC21 and import them into the new system using the retrospective conversion module. All 9,600 imported records had to be verified before we began adding other records into the new software. For the remaining records, we used the Z39.50 protocol to download records from the Library of Congress and the British National Bibliography; the hit rate was between 70–80 percent. The librarian in charge of processing developed a step-by-step procedure manual for downloading records from the BNB and LC databases, making it easier for the staff to assist in the search and downloading of records. Those records that did not have CIP details required manual cataloguing.

Accreditation Standards

There had been interactions between the institution and the Commission for Higher Education (CHE) regarding local accreditation. This was in addition to the continental evangelical accreditation received from the Accrediting Commission for Theological Education in Africa (ACTEA). Part of the requirement of the CHE for the library was that the library classification system had to be the Library of Congress Classification while we were using Dewey Decimal. This requirement extended to all higher learning institutions in the country. With the retrospective conversion exercise, we included the reclassification effort. This meant printing new labels for over 29,000 resources and a complete reorganization of books on library shelves to conform to the new system.

The accrediting body was also quite particular on staffing levels and qualifications. In our case, they required that the head librarian needed to have a minimum of a master's degree training in library science, with adequate numbers of other trained staff. Our head librarian met this qualification; however, she left before the doctoral programs started. It became necessary to recruit or train a successor who would take the process to the next level. The institution decided on further training to prepare the deputy librarian (the author of this article), who had walked very closely with the head librarian, to take over leadership. This meant continuity in the plans without any significant challenges. A lesson learned here was that the library needs to have the head attend planning meetings as well as another promising library staff member. For our case, the deputy had participated in the meetings alongside the head librarian. To meet staff level requirements, the library employed two more qualified staff, one to be in charge of acquisitions and processing, which was earlier managed by the deputy librarian, and another staff member to take care of ICT issues. It had become apparent that the library needed someone to connect with the IT department and champion technology-related issues in the library.

Budget

All mentioned developments – infrastructure, resources, and personnel – depended on the availability of adequate funding. The doctoral programs development committee had been put in place three years before the commencement of the program. The committee mandate included fundraising for library needs to upgrade it to the expected standards. Therefore, the library summarized its needs, and the doctoral committee worked to raise funds. Over the three years of preparation for the two doctoral programs, the library budget was about $500,000. Various individual and corporate donors were identified by the committee and involved in the discussions from the beginning. Donors were grouped according to their interests – this proved very helpful. Some donors required that the institution demonstrate commitment by raising 50 percent of what was requested to receive matching grants. This kept the committee busy in identifying and raising funds to build the base for the matching.

Current Status

The library collection has over the years grown to more than 60,000 volumes of print resources. Subscriptions to several leading databases for ebooks and ejournals supplement the existing print resources. The subscription to electronic resources is primarily through a consortium of higher learning institutions in Kenya. The accrediting commission requires that all higher learning institutions be members of the consortium.

Three more PhD programs have been added on top of the two that started in 2005 –Theology; Inter-Cultural Studies (Missions, World Christianity, Islamics); and General and Applied Linguistics. A further three have been approved by the accrediting body and are offered in 2021. The subsequent doctoral programs have placed less strain on the library as compared to the first two. This shows that an institution needs to get it right the first time – the addition of subsequent programs will be somewhat easier because the institution might not need extra staff and infrastructure, and will only need additional information resources in the areas of specializations. Staffing numbers have not changed dramatically – only three staff members have been added. However, there has been considerable change in professional development: one person has earned a PhD, one a master's degree (with two others having completed programs and awaiting graduation), and concerning in-training, one has a master's, one a diploma, and two have gained on-the-job experience.

Current staffing, with their experience, training, and numbers, has enabled the development of an Information Literacy framework that includes a core subject that is taught to all undergraduate students. Postgraduate students take library seminars for ten weeks covering all aspects of information skills and other library-user interest areas. The user-services librarian always plans classes in information literacy and the general orientation for new doctoral and other graduate cohorts.

Serving doctoral students is not entirely different from serving other students because they all need information and skills on how to find, access, and use the information once it is located. The slight difference is that doctoral students need precise in-depth information and are less sure of exactly what they are looking for.

Challenges and Lessons Learned

The cost of developing the library to offer doctoral programs can be high and requires substantial effort and finances. We were lucky to have a strong doctoral development committee who did well in fundraising. There was a partnership with the Summer Institute of Linguistics in the development of the PhD in Linguistics. However, even with good planning, we encountered challenges that included shipping and clearance logistics. Some books did not arrive at the expected times. A lesson learned was that purchase of resources should be made well in advance before the program starts.

Partnerships and cooperation both within and without the institution helped the library move faster in its preparation for the commencement of the doctoral programs. The inclusion of the librarian at the early stages of the project kept the department abreast of the needs of the program. Visits by professional librarians experienced with doctoral programs was very helpful. Partnership with the Theological Book Network and Langham Literature aided the collection development process that was actively spearheaded internally by faculty in liaison with the librarians. We learned that collection development for the commencement of doctoral programs is a joint and collaborative task. However, we lacked a collection development policy and so did not have guidelines. The policy was drafted during the process and later adopted for implementation.

2. "To Stretch the Imagination": The China Graduate School of Theology Library (Hong Kong)

Dr. Joyce Sun, Associate Professor and Librarian (until July 2021)

Launching of a PhD Program

China Graduate School of Theology (CGST) is an inter-denominational theological school in Hong Kong. It seeks to serve Chinese churches in Hong Kong, mainland China, and overseas by providing theological training at the graduate level for university graduates to become leaders in churches of these regions.

Although the PhD program at CGST was formally launched in 2002, the vision to set up a doctoral program was received and discussed as early as the mid-1990s. Celebrations of the school's 20th anniversary gave this vision even more impetus. Since none of the seminaries in Hong Kong (let alone mainland China) were offering PhD studies at that time, it was hoped that the new program could develop reliable and outstanding theological educators and researchers for China and Asia. Their teaching and writing in Chinese would foster research and theological contextualization on local soil.

Involvement of the Librarian in the Preparation of the Doctoral Program

The CGST library's preparation for the new PhD program benefitted greatly from two aspects: the school's administration devoted some of its budget to upgrading the library's facilities and enlarging its holdings; and their librarian was a faculty member at the school at the same time. Because of this, the librarian had access to the discussions on and plans for the forthcoming program, and he commenced preparatory works well before the program's inception. To meet the accreditation requirements set out by the Asia Theological Association, the first thing that the library needed to do was to expand its collection of academic journals and non-English books.

Since the librarian was a doctorate degree holder himself, he was familiar with the research process that doctoral students would go through and the level of research materials they would need to complete their PhD dissertations. At the same time, he hoped to equip the library's doctoral collection with titles relevant to students' research topics and needs when they arrived. Acquisitions made by the library at this stage mainly concentrated on general research and reference works. Some funds were held back for necessary acquisitions when the doctoral student intake would actually have taken place and their topics would be known. The adopted pace and steps taken by the CGST library closely followed and largely depended on the planning and implementation process of the school. By 2001, before the first doctoral student intake in 2003, the library had acquired 399 non-English books as part of its doctoral collection (many of them second-hand).

Image 3: Entrance to the CGST Library

As the school did not belong to any denomination and did not have any major long-term funding sources, its resources, whether financial or otherwise, needed to be utilized with good care and caution. Resources allocated by the library for the initial setup of its doctoral holdings were mainly targeted at the research interests of potential candidates. Since many of the faculty at that time were Karl Barth experts and it was to be expected that accepted students would work in similar areas, the library spent a substantial part of its budget on acquiring books relevant to Karl Barth research.

The expansion of the doctoral holdings was significantly aided by the sponsorship of the Overseas Council International for Theological Education (OCI), a Christian organization aiming to advance the academic excellence of theological schools in the Majority World. The school also obtained a matching grant to develop the doctoral research collection, so it had to engage in fundraising efforts to secure the matching grant. By 2006, the library owned more than 1,000 non-English books in addition to its English and Chinese collections. Its journal collection also rose from 413 issues (including Chinese and English titles) in 2001 to 514 issues in 2006, together with the addition of four electronic full-text journal databases.

To utilize available funding most effectively, the library has throughout, and up to the present, adopted the strategy of limiting its holdings to works specific to, or related to, Christianity. Students engaging in interdisciplinary research in which the necessary research materials are not available at the CGST library are encouraged to seek assistance from universities where they studied previously or at the Hong Kong Baptist University library nearby.[1] In 2013 a program was launched that awards a joint PhD degree between CGST and the University of Edinburgh (UoE) – the students enrolled in that program can also use UoE library resources. In this way, the CGST library can concentrate on those needs that students cannot satisfy through other venues.

One-to-One Service Model

The school's annual doctoral student intake remains steadily at single digits, therefore the CGST library manages to serve every doctoral research student on a one-to-one basis. When the first two doctoral students were admitted in 2003 – one engaged in Karl Barth research and the other followed a topic from the Old Testament book of Leviticus – the library consciously expanded its holdings in these two areas. When new students shift to other areas of study with the approval of their supervisors and the Postgraduate Committee, the library accordingly adjusts its acquisition strategy to cater to such changes. The fact that the librarian happens to be a member of the Postgraduate Committee also serves at an early stage for the library to become aware of an incoming doctoral student's research needs and their particular fields so that acquisitions can commence and be adjusted even before the student arrives.

Besides providing relevant book holdings, the CGST library emphasizes meeting students' personal needs and offering its space as a convenient and comfortable place for students to do individual research. Despite its constant shortage of physical space, the library allows students to choose their desks. Desks next to bookshelves with materials on students' particular research interests will likely be their pick. Furthermore, personal lockers are provided for students to keep borrowed books without carrying them to and from home.

The provision of these tailor-made services by no means implies that the library is indiscriminately acceding to student requests without supervision. Since all student requests for books and journals have to be approved by the librarian, the librarian can always screen these requests and make sure they

---

1. For the mutual issuances of Institutional Reader's Tickets between CGST library and the Hong Kong Baptist University library, please refer to the section on Inter-Library Collaboration below.

are relevant and necessary for each student's studies. If in doubt, the librarian will contact the appropriate supervisor for clarification and/or adjustments to the request list.

Image 4: Computer Facility

Facing the Digital Age

Rapid advances in technology and the increasing appearance of electronic resources have done great service to the CGST library in recent decades. Situated in Hong Kong, where land prices are notoriously high, the library continually has to deal with a shortage of space. The availability of electronic materials allows the library to expand its collection with a minimum usage of physical space, which releases space to meet more urgent needs, such as the provision of study areas, and the installation of more computing and copying facilities.

If a certain work is available both in print and digital versions, the library will give priority to the digital format. If the budget allows, the library is also inclined to acquire prestigious online databases, such as the Dead Sea Scroll Electronic Library, The Digital Karl Barth Library, and the Bulletin of the Institute of Modern History, Academia Sinica, through which renowned but voluminous collections can be accessed online by students without using any physical space in the library. The library has now launched a process of putting its physical journals in closed stacks and replacing them with digital versions (if available) so the library can release these stacks to hold other items. While expanding its capacity to house the ever-increasing number of publications, the library is at the same time somewhat relieved of the urgency to locate extension space or even move to larger premises.

Image 5: Doctoral Student Desk

In addition, the services of the CGST library for research students have been further enhanced by the introduction of digital research tools. The library has managed to purchase RefWorks, a bibliography and database manager, to help students create and organize their own personal resources in the research process and import citations and generate bibliographies for their dissertations. Another tool especially provided for research students is Adobe Acrobat Pro, which allows them to convert documents and images to PDF or Word format, and import quotations to their research papers.

To guide students through the matrix of digital tools and resources available at the library, the CGST library team provides orientation and instruction to each beginning doctoral student, once again on a one-to-one basis. This personal guidance proves to be particularly valuable to students from mainland China and those who accomplished previous studies in other institutions. Such one-to-one companionship lasts throughout a student's whole course of doctoral pursuit at CGST. Since students have their own desks inside the library, many are well acquainted with the library staff. Whenever they have queries and problems locating resources or using any library facilities, the staff can immediately assist them. The library team is constantly present at their side and welcomes requests, ranging from finding a specific piece of work to advising on how and where to locate materials relevant to a particular research topic.

Besides one-to-one contacts, doctoral students at CGST can also improve their information proficiency and research skills by watching video tutorials posted on the library's webpage or, on their own initiative, attend training sessions and workshops organized by the library for the orientation of all students. Indeed, the CGST library team plays an indispensable role in providing information services and promoting the information literacy of the school as a whole. Sometimes, it even extends suggestions and advice to the school's administration on the latest development of research tools and on up-to-date versions of equipment. The digital microfiche reader and scanner with optical character recognition (OCR) function, now installed at the library, is one typical example of the contribution that the library team had towards improving students' research experience in their doctoral pursuits. The machine was purchased on the library's advice in 2019 when the school obtained funding to acquire the International Missionary Council Archives, 1910–1961, which was available only in microfiche format.

Staff Development Strategy

It is evident that to facilitate students' information competency in doing research and accessing materials, and to advise the school administration on recent trends of research skills and facilities, the library team must first themselves be well versed in these skills and facilities and keep themselves abreast of the latest developments and innovations.

When CGST had its first doctoral student intake in 2003, among the five members of the library team, only one had a master's degree relevant to library management. There were students who once questioned the professional qualifications of the library staff. Now in 2020, three of the team members, including the associate and the assistant librarians, hold a Master of Information Studies degree. Besides information literacy, research skills, and collections, their areas of training further include philosophies of research and learning behaviors in digital environments. Though not having a master's degree in library management, the other two members of the team have received professional training in specific areas of library operation, including knowledge management and conservation of books and documents.

One factor contributing to this significant increase in professional qualifications within the library team is that the school recognizes library management as a professional activity. Every library staff member is encouraged to engage in part-time studies relevant to his or her job. On the librarian's recommendation, he or she can apply for support from the school, whether in the form of a financial subsidy or study leave, to advance in studies. Upon graduation, the new professional qualification will be recognized and become a factor to be taken into consideration when reviewing remuneration and job positions.

Having dealt with the question of professional qualification, the next issue that the CGST library may need to address is the theological literacy of library staff. After all, CGST is a theology school. Adequate knowledge of the subjects students engage in is indeed beneficial when the team needs to provide assistance in locating materials relevant to students' topics. However, engaging in theological studies often goes together with one's own calling and spiritual aspirations. So the library can only encourage and persuade, praying that one day some of its team members will have the vision to take up this pursuit.

Inter-Library Collaboration

With the rapid changes of information technologies, research skills, education practices, and publishing behavior, and together with the ever-increasing amount of new resources, tools, and publications, libraries can hardly work alone and, at the same time, keep abreast with all these trends and developments. The problem is particularly acute for theological libraries in Hong Kong and mainland China, which usually have relatively modest budgets. The advantages of cooperation and working in concert with other institutions to meet student needs are obvious.

The CGST library is currently a member of seven library associations including the American Theological Library Association, Association of British Theological and Philosophical Libraries, Forum of Asian Theological Librarians, and Hong Kong Library Association. Participation in these associations serves to provide platforms for the library to engage in international exchange and share information on library and ministry development. The library team is, from time to time, invited to attend presentations and workshops organized by these associations to keep track of the latest developments, such as library management, copyright, metadata, and cataloguing practices. The library is even eligible for discounted prices when purchasing electronic resources through these channels.

In addition, the CGST library has an arrangement with the Hong Kong Baptist University library in which Institutional Reader's Tickets are mutually issued to each other's users so that CGST students have access to the collection of the university and can make photocopies of resources. This arrangement is particularly pertinent to the needs of doctoral students doing inter-disciplinary research. They can obtain resources on sociology, psychology, political science, and even linguistics and history, without affecting the library budget.

Image 6: Reading Hall CGST

Last but not at all least, CGST has since 1997 formally become a member of the Ecumenical Information Network (EIN) in Hong Kong. EIN is a network of Hong Kong theological libraries formed in 1995 for inter-library cooperation on resource sharing and electronic information development. The network consists of five members who share the same proxy server and union catalogue, so that students of any member institution can, with one click, view resources held by all five. This is possible through the Primo Discovery Tool Service, also jointly purchased by EIN members in 2013. The EIN Union Catalogue is now the most extensive theological library catalogue in Hong Kong and the largest Chinese theological library catalogue in the world. Furthermore, all EIN members use the same cataloging system and handbook so that each item's MARC (machine-readable cataloguing) record is standardized and one library's MARC record can be used by the other four without duplication of effort.

Indeed, besides mutual services such as ILL and Document-Delivery Service, whereby expensive books and journals acquired by one library can be shared with the other four, cooperation among EIN members is varied and visible. We have regular meetings four to five times a year, in which issues on cataloguing, library system, joint-ventures, and cooperation opportunities are explored and discussed. Each library representative takes a turn annually to coordinate the meeting and be responsible for the communication, liaison among EIN members, and suppliers, other organizations, and units.

Since EIN's establishment, its members have jointly undertaken significant projects, exemplifying how cooperation among institutions can reap significant benefits for their participants. The acquisition of Primo Discovery Tool Service, and the employment of a system administrator at shared costs, have enabled each member, including the CGST library, to provide faster access to scholarly materials and new contents with minimum pressure on its budget. Cooperation also allows EIN members to acquire prestigious collections at an affordable price, such as the Loeb Classical Library database. At present, each EIN member is committed to spending a fixed amount of money every year purchasing electronic books to be used jointly by all the members. The larger the aggregate amount being spent, the greater the bargaining power EIN members have in negotiating for better prices.

Furthermore, collaboration among EIN members can also take the form of applying for funding under the network's name to enrich their holdings and facilities. Besides having more electronic books and databases added to their collections, EIN's funding in the past actually enabled its members to develop a Chinese full-text journal database and have their old and rare books digitalized.

CGST has received much joy and is very blessed through collaboration with other theological libraries in Hong Kong. Insofar as theological libraries are willing to share and stretch their imagination, the forms and possibilities of cooperation and joint-efforts can be far broader than originally perceived.

3. "Excellence Is a Journey": The South Asia Institute of Advanced Christian Studies Library (Bangalore)

Dr. Yesan Sellan, Chief Librarian

Introduction

It was in the summer of 1981 in Kodaikanal, a hill station in Southern India, that the idea of starting an evangelical mission-focused higher theological training institute emerged out of a conversation over tea between Dr. Graham

Houghton and Dr. Bruce Nicholls, who had come as missionaries to India.[2] The South Asia Institute of Advanced Christian Studies (SAIACS) was founded in 1982 with the conviction that churches in India needed something more than just another Bible college or seminary. The Institute was intended to provide excellent programs of graduate theological education in response to a widespread need for reputable training in Christian leadership in India and throughout South Asia. As there was no real infrastructure within which to do this, it was suggested that the degree be offered by the newly formed Association of Evangelical Theological Education in India (AETEI). Dr. Houghton, then the dean, set up a two-year course, and classes began in June 1982 amid enthusiastic support from church leaders and prospective students. Initially, they planned to wind up the program after the first batch of students had graduated. But as applications continued to come in, it was decided to repeat the course of studies and move the program from Madras to Bangalore. In 1984, the program disengaged from the AETEI, and in 1985 SAIACS was registered separately as an educational trust in Bangalore with Dr. Houghton as the principal.[3]

SAIACS was started out of a need to address concerns about "brain-drain" (Indian students who do not return to India after their studies in Western universities), about the irrelevance of Western theological education for the South Asian context, and for a better financial stewardship.

In the beginning, the library

In the year 1982 – when SAIACS was first in Chennai, then Madras – the library holdings counted two hundred books and a few periodicals, which belonged to the founding principal Dr. Houghton. The entire library holdings were held on one small wooden shelf. This bookshelf is still kept in the chief librarian's office as a reminder of the library's beginnings. One of the students was in charge of counting the books every day and taking care of the library. In 1984, the SAIACS programs were moved to Bangalore. Since SAIACS had no property, it began in a rented building in Bangalore. The principal's office was in a garage, and the library and reception were both in one room. Classes were held in several houses. The visit of an accreditation team from the Asia Theological Association in 1983 encouraged the school to continue to offer the programs and strongly recommended that the library be further developed.

---

2. South Asian Institute of Advanced Christian Studies, ed., *SAIACS: The First Thirty Years* (Bangalore: SAIACS Press, 2012).

3. https://www.saiacs.org.

Books from various sources were acquired, and the collection grew. Around this time, an interesting development took place in the history of theological libraries in Bangalore: a formal meeting of five seminary libraries took place in 1985, which eventually became one of the successful library networks in India, called the Joint Library Committee (JLC). SAIACS was one of the founding members of the JLC. This formal arrangement helped SAIACS students to use resources available in the member libraries of the JLC.

Image 7: SAIACS Library

In the year 1987, the library resources grew to seven thousand with hopes to move to a new campus in early 1989. In 1987, during the planning period for acquiring a location on the outskirts of Bangalore, SAIACS was temporarily moved to a Bible college closer to the property. The SAIACS library holdings were kept separately in this college, and a separate counter was used for issuing books. A student librarian cared for the collection during his break times. Students occasionally commuted to other college libraries in the city to use their resources. Library development was gradual and steady. The founding principal was very instrumental in the library's development, and faculty members were encouraged to recommend acquisitions of books for the library. Faculty members often visited local book stores, publishers' warehouses, and book exhibitions – these were some of the few endeavors which supported the growth of the library.

After acquiring the new property, the new campus's administrative building was completed and dedicated in January 1989. The library was shifted from the adjacent college, where it had been temporarily housed for a few months, into one of the large rooms on the first floor. It was used as a library and a classroom, but eventually, the weight of the books developed some cracks in the wall. So, quickly the library was moved to the ground floor. At that time, the library added a few important reference resources, like Biblical Illustrator, pulpit commentaries, and others on mission and pastoral theology to meet the growing needs of academic programs. The college administration felt the need for a separate library building that could hold a collection of maximum 100,000 books. The planned-for separate building for the library was built and dedicated in March 1993. At present the library collection has grown to over 65,000 books.

Start of a PhD Program

Though SAIACS was started to offer a missiological program at the master's degree level, from 1987 onwards, there proceeded to be a series of discussions and plans at the board level of SAIACS to explore the possibility of offering a doctoral degree program, including partnerships with overseas universities. Doctor of Missiology (DMiss) and Doctor of Ministry (DMin) degree programs were introduced in 1988. These programs are primarily intended to support practicing mission leaders and pastors. Persistent efforts by the principal and partnerships with various organizations have helped the library to grow.

In 1990 the library collection crossed the 10,000 mark, acquiring about 1,500 books annually. Through overseas donors' funds, the library collection soon increased to 15,000 books and 165 periodical subscriptions.

The year 1997 was an important milestone in the life of SAIACS, because the University of Mysore, one of the state universities in Karnataka, provided official recognition for SAIACS as a research center to offer PhDs in specialized Christianity through the Department of Christian Studies at the university. This affirmation helped SAIACS to offer a PhD program recognized by a state university in India. By this time, the library resources were also expanded, and acquisition of new books was possible with the help of recommendations from the faculty. At this time, the collection reached 20,000 with subscriptions to 180 journals. One of the well-wishers of SAIACS, Mrs. Margaret Falkowski, came forward to subscribe to journals on behalf of SAIACS and mail them once every six months. This arrangement continues today. It has saved the library budget a great deal of shipping costs and limited the financial burden on the institution. In 1997 another noteworthy library development was the visit of a retired librarian, Mr. William Dale Ward from Canada, on the advice of Prof. David Sherbino in the Tyndale University College and Seminary, Toronto.

This visit facilitated arrangements for Tyndale College to begin helping with subscriptions to electronic resources for the SAIACS library.

Dale Ward's involvement, being himself a librarian with much experience in library software solutions, has played a very important role in the growth of the SAIACS library. In regular visits, Dr. Ward provided library staff training in the use of the internet and the procurement of library software. Following the appointment in 2004 of the current librarian, Dale Ward did not feel the need for further visits. However, he has continued to mentor and guide the librarian in connecting with several library associations and libraries.

Application of Information Technologies

Apart from offering regular library services to students and faculty, the library was also called upon to help in typing students' assignments. One of the library staff was even asked to help with correcting grammar and spelling mistakes in the students' assignments. As time went on, the need to introduce computers was obvious, and the year 1995 was an important landmark when the first ten computers were purchased. The computers were primarily intended for students so that they could produce their assignments themselves, which greatly relieved the library staff. Since there were only ten computers available for word processing, students booked their slots and were sometimes seen even late at night completing their assignments.

During this time the acquisition of books on CD-ROMs was considered remarkable as hundreds of books could be stored and retrieved from one single disc. Plans for developing resources on biblical studies, pastoral theology, and for the religion department were implemented in this way, and several important commentaries and other textbooks were made available on CD-ROM. Around this period, the founding principal, being a historian, showed much interest in acquiring microfilm and microfiche with records on early mission and church history. These additions further strengthened the library collection in becoming a research library.

The need for automation was recognized, and the introduction of an integrated library management system was initiated in 1998. As part of this process, a team visited several university and theological libraries in India and finally presented a proposal. The team consisted of the SAIACS librarian and an experienced visiting librarian from Canada. In the end, software developed by Algorithms Pvt Ltd, Pune, called SLIM++, was selected, as it was also used in another seminary in Pune. The introduction of a computerized system in the library led to the development of its IT infrastructure in 2000.

Open-source software development has received significant attention and appreciation among Majority World libraries. The arrival of several open-source products, such as Koha, NewGenLib, and others, has caused significant changes in India's libraries. SAIACS library planned its migration to Koha from SLIM++ software in 2013. The migration was not an easy process, yet with much perseverance, data transfer was successfully completed within two years. Attending workshops and implementing a demo-server helped in training the staff in the use of Koha. Off-campus access to the library catalogue and integration with electronic resources became possible. After much discussion and the evaluation of various products, we identified OCLC's EZproxy as helpful to support off-campus access. The implementation of EZproxy was timely, and during the pandemic period, students and faculty have been able to access our resources from anywhere.

Collection Development

The SAIACS library acquires resources based on the needs expressed by the faculty members for meeting course requirements and on the needs of thesis research students. An official library committee was not formed until 2001. However, most of the development plans and ideas emerged from faculty and staff retreats in Joel Committee meetings.[4] This encouraged faculty members to brainstorm and present ideas, including ideas for library development. Faculty members were always encouraged to suggest the purchase of books for the library. The principal was proactively involved in adding resources to the library regularly and made the final decisions. There was no collection development policy as such; however, with the involvement of faculty members and the principal, there were hardly any unwanted or unused resources added to the library.

The partnership with Overseas Council International (OCI) and OC of New Zealand and Australia was significant in the growth of SAIACS. This partnership helped with the building of several core collections of books as well as assistance in staff development. The decision to form a regional research center in collaboration with Theological Book Network (TBN) and Scholar Leaders International (SLI) has further significantly enhanced special collections focused on biblical studies, religion, theology, and pastoral theology. Book donations from retired professors were another major source of acquisitions for the SAIACS library. The founding principal and his wife always

---

4. The "Joel Committee" consists of staff and faculty members and normally meets during the annual all-SAIACS retreat to brainstorm ideas and plan developments for the future.

spoke with the professors nearing retirement and inquired about a possible donation of their personal libraries. These personal libraries have always held some of the best collections of books. One noteworthy donation came from Prof. Robert Eric Frykenberg. It adds significant value to the library collection as it comprises one of the finest collections of resources on South Asian history, mission, and religious studies. In December 2019 Dr. Patricia Harrison from Australia gifted her personal library collection to SAIACS library. This donation included 6,000 titles in the areas of missiology and intercultural studies. This collection had considerable biblical and theological resources to support the study on religions, theology, sociology, and others.

The support of Langham Literature has also contributed to library growth through their library grant and additional books. Standing orders with select publishers in India have helped to regularly add Indian publications. Lack of collection development has been a challenge in later years and the library plans to adopt a new collection development policy. As of today, the SAIACS library subscribes to 200 print journals, has over 65,000 books, has 500 microfiche, and provides access to online databases such as ATLA Religion Database with Serials, JSTOR, Global Digital Theological library, and others.

Electronic Resources

In order to reap the benefits of new technologies and of digital resources and to address the needs of academic programs, the SAIACS library, in partnership with Tyndale Seminary, Toronto, started a CD-ROM subscription to the ATLA Religion Database in 2003. ATLA had introduced a special program through which a North American library could gain a second subscription to the ATLA Religion Database for a reduced price and donate it to a Majority World library. Tyndale's support in procuring such a subscription for SAIACS was very important. Later in 2008 we migrated to an online subscription to the ATLA Religion Database with Serials on the EBSCO platform. ATLA(S) offers full-text articles from over 360 journals. Through the Christian Library Consortia of ACL, of which the SAIACS librarian is a member, the library acquired 1,400 ebooks at a discounted price. A significant collection of ebooks on pastoral theology, religion, and biblical studies was added through this arrangement.

SAIACS was the first library in India to subscribe to premier religious and theological online databases. Meanwhile the library has also upgraded its CD-ROM version of the Theological Journal Library to the Logos program. As of 2020, the Logos system in the SAIACS library has nearly 4,000 electronic resources. Also, since 2015, the library started its subscription to JSTOR through membership in a national consortium called INFLIBNET (Information Library Network). JSTOR offers full-text articles from 2,000 journals. Subscription to the Global Digital Theological Library has further enhanced digital resources available for students and faculty members.

Library Staff and Committee

Until 2001, there was no library committee in place. Before that, most of the library matters were discussed and decided in the faculty meeting, which seemed easier for decision making and implementation. Library staff were taken into confidence when major decisions needed to be made. Only two trained librarians were on staff then. Two other assistants were employed to support library services. I joined the team in 2004 and introduced current standards for library services. At present, the library staff is comprised of four professional librarians, one with a doctorate degree in library and information science. As part of the support rendered to other libraries, the SAIACS library designed a three-month certificate program called Theological Librarianship. Through this program SAIACS has trained over fifty librarians. Starting in 2021, SAIACS plans to offer an online theological librarianship course at the postgraduate level. As far as library staff is concerned, SAIACS has always been supportive of developing and enhancing of their knowledge with the current developments in the field of library information science (LIS). Financial support is made available for staff to attend conferences, workshops, and refresher courses. One of the assistant librarians has been trained on archives management at the Asbury Theological Seminary, Kentucky, USA, and the current librarian was supported to pursue doctoral studies in LIS.

Support for Doctoral Students

The library has introduced special reading cubicles, or research carrels, for MTh and doctoral students. This helps students to enjoy a quiet, undisturbed reading space. Students are allowed to hold a certain number of books in their carrels for quick access. Other students who need to refer to books used by thesis students approach the library staff for assistance. At the beginning of each academic year, students are given orientation and training on library use. In addition, thesis writing students are permitted to make recommendations to the library for acquisition of new books. This helps the library discern needs and add useful titles to its collection. Faculty advisors for doctoral students always work closely with library staff to ensure that doctoral students' needs are met. Library training is offered to the doctoral and master's thesis students during their proposal seminars which helps the library staff to present specific user-focused training to support their writing projects. Throughout the thesis writing process, the chief librarian has regular personal interactions with doctoral students to know their progress in thesis writing as well as to identify their information needs. The personal interactions have always helped the library to add important resources and update the collections in various departments. Faculty advisors insist thesis students meet with the chief librarian regularly to gain access to needed resources for their research projects.

Inter-Library Networks

To ensure timely access to resources needed by students through ILL, SAIACS is currently a member of several associations, such as the Joint Library Committee (JLC), national library association of India, ATLA, ACL, and ForATL. The union catalogue of JLC has over one million bibliographic records. It facilitates students' access to resources available in other libraries. The ILL arrangement through JLC is one of the finest models in India. Under this arrangement, member libraries are responsible for the safe return of books borrowed from other member libraries of JLC.

SAIACS entered into an MoU with Asbury Theological Seminary in 2012. This facilitated SAIACS library to grow strategically in equipping library staff training and access to digital content without any infringement of copyrights. Our library staff, Mr. Prasada Rao, was sent to Asbury Theological Seminary to get trained on archives and other practices followed in preservation and conservation of rare materials. The vision of this arrangement is to support each other's acquisition of resources published in India and Asia that are not readily available in North America. The relationship with Asbury enhanced SAIACS library collection development, staff skill development, and availability to inter-library loan services.

Through special arrangements with several other libraries and librarians in the US, the SAIACS library is able to procure articles, chapters, and conference papers for its doctoral and master's level thesis students.

Learning Experience

I am very glad to have been part of the SAIACS library since 2004. I consider it an honor and privilege to serve the needs of research scholars. It is purely by God's grace and strength that we have been able to elevate the standards of the SAIACS library on par with any research library. It is a continuous process; excellence is not a destination but rather a journey. My dream for the library is to always maintain high standards and be a role model for other libraries. I continue to network with colleagues across the globe who sharpen my skills and ideas. Plans are underway to implement discovery services and an institutional repository for SAIACS. Also, the SAIACS library would like to engage with indigenous mission agencies in India to hold the digital repository of their mission archives and records in order to support indigenous scholarship and preserve those records for future generations.

4. "A Missionary in and of Itself": The John Smyth Library of the International Baptist Theological Study Centre (Amsterdam)

Pieter van Wingerden, Librarian

In June 2014, it was finally happening. After a long period of preparation, the removal trucks filled to the brim with books and shelving were rolling out of the grounds of the International Baptist Theological Seminary in Jeneralka, Prague. Under the watchful eyes of the transition manager, David McMillan, and the head librarian, Zdenko S. Širka, the trucks arrived in Amsterdam to unload a 41,000-volume library into their new premises. It took several weeks to assemble the shelving, unpack, and shelve the books in their appropriate places. When I first walked into the library on the third floor of a regular office building on 3 August 2014, I was struck by the otherworldliness of it. For the next three years, this nondescript office building would be the home of a veritable treasure chest of seventy years of European Baptist history. Since then, we have moved across the street into a building that used to be known as the John Smyth Memorial Church. The print library, that in 2019 was baptized the John Smyth Library in remembrance of the original name of the church, sits on the floor above the church hall. The church still serves as the meeting place for several local and regional congregations and offers a home to the European Baptist Federation, the Dutch Baptist Union, the Dutch Baptist Seminary, and ourselves.

I had some experience working in a library in a mission context, but I felt like a greenhorn when Zdenko used the next couple of days to give me a crash course in the inner workings of this library. From learning the shelving system (Dewey Decimal System with Cutter numbers) to cataloguing books (in MARC21 following LC patterns), I was soon deeply immersed in a new world that is mostly hidden from view. In the same week, Zdenko went back home, and I was left to fend for myself in a newly founded institution.

Image 8: IBTSC Library windows (second floor)

In the course of the next few years, I learned a lot about our heritage: how we were founded in 1949 in Rüschlikon-Switzerland as a Marshall-plan-like mission of the Foreign Mission Board of the Southern Baptist Convention; how we started as an international seminary with the goal of training European Baptist pastors and leaders; how it was a place of embodied European reconciliation after a devastating war; how through the decades more and more European Baptist unions were able to set up their seminaries; how we moved to Eastern Europe in the mid-1990s to be closer to those who most needed our education; how financial constraints led us to leave our beautiful, but costly premises in Prague. We have offered various degrees during the 65+ years of our existence: bachelor's and master's level in Rüschlikon-Switzerland; master's level and a very successful Certificate in Applied Theology (CAT) program in Prague. The doctoral studies adventure started only in 1999 in partnership with the University of Wales (UoW). After a final and decisive visitation, the UoW decided to validate MTh, MPhil, and PhD programs taught at IBTS. To ensure effective preparation for doctoral studies, a Postgraduate Certificate program was started in 2007. This program, upon successful completion, made it possible for our students from very diverse educational backgrounds to enroll in the doctoral program.

Unfortunately, the sources do not tell if the library played any role in the discussions leading up to the foundation of a PhD program. I did not inherit any strategic library documents, so I am inclined to think that there was no detailed work done on the implications that starting a PhD would have for the development of the library. Reports from my predecessors confirm this impression. History does not tell me why the library was not properly considered during these developments.

The joy of having our own doctoral studies program did not last long. The University of Wales was quite unexpectedly dissolved in 2011 and, with it, our PhD program. Provisions were made to allow current students to continue, but no new students would be accepted. This left IBTS with a massive problem. In combination with the financial challenges that the institution faced at the time, the decision was made to move away from Prague. After careful consideration, Amsterdam was chosen for a new home. In June 2013, an agreement was signed with the Vrije Universiteit Amsterdam (VU), who would be the new validating partner for the PhD program.

The current PhD program includes the following components: a 30-ECTS Postgraduate Certificate, the formulation of a doctoral research proposal, and the completion of a dissertation. The one-year Postgraduate Certificate is validated through the European Council for Theological Education. The VU recognizes it for acceptance to their Graduate School of the Faculty of Religion and Theology. Students receive a face-to-face introduction to library resources when they first arrive on campus. Each year the students return for a six-day annual colloquium in January where they present their work, receive peer and supervisor comments, and work in the physical library. Throughout the year, they have access to electronic resources through IBTSC's library and the VU library.

As a new librarian of a new institution with a new partner for a new doctoral program, I had to consider many aspects. The first problem I encountered was how to serve students whom I had never met and whom I would normally meet only once a year during a short annual PhD colloquium. The 41,000 print volumes were not going to be of much use to them most of the year. In Prague, we were part of two different consortia that provided access to the ATLA Religion Database® with ATLASerials® and EBSCO's Academic Search Complete. The international move made us ineligible for further participation in the Czech government-supported consortium, so we lost access to Academic Search Complete (participation in a similar Dutch consortium was out of our financial reach). EBSCO allowed us to hold on to the Czech ATLA-subscription to smooth the transition. We also subscribed to a small ProQuest journal collection and two ebook collections from academic publishers (Oxford University Press and Cambridge University Press).

In and of itself, these four digital collections were not bad as a complementary set of resources. But as a substitute for unlimited access to a print collection, it was a relatively meagre, perhaps even an emaciated alternative. My first task was to ensure that our distance-learning students would be served with access to ample electronic resources. We were helped by our association with the VU since our students were eligible to receive a VUnet ID that provided remote access to their entire digital holdings. However, the process of getting students registered at VU is somewhat cumbersome, and not all students are as digitally gifted as they need to be.

Blessings came in the guise of an American mission-driven visionary whom I bumped into in September 2016 at the 45th annual BETH conference (Bibliothèques Européennes de Théologie = European Theological Libraries). The conference presentations were centered around the theme of open access. One of the speakers was Dr. Thomas E. Phillips, dean of libraries of Claremont School of Theology in California, who talked about the Open Library of Humanities. Tom had just launched a new initiative, the Digital Theological Library (DTL). The Digital Theological Library is a "co-owned, born-digital library of religious and theological studies." Every owner school contributes an annual fee based on their student full-time equivalency (FTE), and their patrons are given remote access to all contents of this digital library. Since our student numbers are relatively low, and all are part-time, this is a very affordable solution for our library. Our students have remote access to over 600,000 ebooks and millions of articles in various areas of study.

As other areas are mainly covered through DTL and electronic resources, in our collection development policy, we have designated our print library as a Baptist research library (IFLA Conspectus Level 4). The ambition is to grow it in our niche specialty of Baptist identity, mission, and practice in the geographical region of the EBF (Europe, Middle East, and Central Asia) and beyond.

If I summarized my role now, it would broadly fall under three categories:

1. Reference assistance

2. Acquisitions

3. (Inter)national contacts

Reference assistance

My first and foremost task is to assist research students. We currently have thirty-seven students at various stages of their PhD journey. They all get access to the DTL, so it's my job to instruct them on how to use it. I am also their go-to person when they hit a dead end with obtaining resources. As co-owner of the DTL, I have privileges that allow me to request new additions to the library, and this has been tremendously helpful in many cases. However, sometimes it's not possible to acquire a whole journal for the sake of being able to access one issue. Through international networks I have been able to source almost everything students need for their research. As independent research students, they can feel isolated. I see my role in taking away their worries in the area of resourcing and referencing.

Acquisitions

We want the John Smyth Library to serve as a European Baptist research library. Our main acquisition focus is on materials by and about Baptists from all European Baptist communities in English and other languages. This is then complemented by an exhaustive collection of Baptist Studies monographs and journals. The goal is to provide one central place in Europe where we document the Baptist faith story in Europe. Future plans include the digitization of rare and old Baptist materials from various European countries to make them available in open access with a full-text search capability, which will simplify doctoral and other research into the history of Baptist identity, mission, and practice. My task is to ensure this material is available in-house before the researchers even realize they need it.

(Inter)national contacts

Our library is embedded in an international library landscape. Because our focus is on European Baptist studies, our main networks are in Europe. We are connected, in various capacities, to the European, Dutch, British, German, French, Eurasian, and North American theological library networks. This has led to significant partnerships that have proven to be of benefit to our research students.

Reflecting on the principles outlined in this book, it seems that everything came to us in the wrong order. The institution took steps and changed programs without involving the library in strategic thinking. (Being book lovers, they, however, allocated a comfortable budget for book purchases.) This lack of involvement left the librarian in the unfortunate circumstance of 41,000 books with no students on the ground to use them. In hindsight, all our strategic developments were born from an uneven situation where no library strategy was developed when the institution changed direction. Some of the mishaps could, however, be remedied later.

From the five areas listed in this book, I believe we have our house in order when it comes to the first three.

Area 1: Integration of Library in Planning a Doctoral Program

We are in a luxurious position in that we have successfully remedied the problem of a print library without students on the grounds. Thanks to the DTL and to a satisfactory budget, we have been able to turn the situation to our advantage. We offer extensive electronic resources to our students while at the same time funneling our print acquisitions budget into a core collection. Because the doctoral program is at the heart of the institution, the library has the doctoral students as its central focus.

Area 2: Partnerships and Collaboration

Our institution is still a very small one. We have two full-time and three part-time staff, supported by a varying group of adjuncts, contractors, and volunteers. This allows us to keep in close connection with each other and hold the library in the center of things. Because it is a single-staff library, it is of tantamount importance to me to ground myself in the national and international library community. Close relationships with several denominational theological universities in the Netherlands have proven very rewarding. We share a union catalog with two other universities and bring an academic evangelical and free-church theological perspective to the mostly reformed table. Without our international relations, we would not have become a co-owner of the DTL, which would have made life quite a bit more difficult for our research students.

Area 3: Collection Development and Management

Over the past few years, I have done a lot of work in the areas of collection development, cataloguing, and electronic resources. For the last four years, we have a collection development policy that also gave rise to a long-term strategic plan focusing on safeguarding Baptist heritage for the future. We migrated into a new catalog set-up that has made our collection visible on the WorldCat level (www.worldcat.org). It also made it possible for us to tap into a national and international ILL network.

The next two areas still deserve quite some attention in our institution.

Area 4: The Role(s) of Library Personnel

I am a part-time librarian running a whole library by myself. That puts severe constraints on my time and does not allow me to develop everything that I would like to see developed. Sometimes even the piles of to-be-catalogued materials can be disheartening, but I'm sure this happens in better-staffed libraries as well.

Area 5: Information Literacy in Doctoral Program(s)

Since our students come with a master's degree, I can expect a certain level of information literacy. But the fact that the student body ranges from all over the world leads to very diverse levels of information literacy among our students. I tend to initiate the research students into the secrets of a library during their first Post-Graduate Certificate week in Amsterdam and try to deal with some issues topically. Still, we could profit from a more thorough and systematic approach to helping students keep on top of things.

Conclusion

I am very excited about the future of the IBTS Centre and the John Smyth Library. We are in a much better place now than when I first walked through the doors in August 2014. As this story shows, the institution has failed on multiple occasions to take the principles outlined in this book into account when thinking about its future. We have found ourselves in precarious situations where there was no match between student needs and our services. I'm delighted that the library has developed to the required standards in several areas, but the work is not finished. May our resources, through the work that is being done by our research students, contribute to the building of God's kingdom. In that sense, every theological library is a missionary in and of itself.

5. What Do We See?: Some Reflections on the "Transition Stories"

Katharina Penner, EAAA Coordinator for Library Development

1. Planning a doctoral program: with – not without – the library! As the above stories from institutions in different parts of the world amply demonstrate, the introduction and operation of a doctoral program in a Majority World theological school requires concerted effort and presumes a long strategic process.[5] The doctoral program will affect all areas of a school's operation and so, much attention to systematic planning is of benefit. The library is no exception – its development toward quality service for the doctoral program requires a carefully thought through approach which cannot happen overnight. The provision of research resources is vital to doctoral programs; however, strangely, library teams are often not included in the relevant program development committees.

The rationale behind such a decision often assumes that the academic leadership is adequately qualified to think and decide "for" the library. However, as the principles in the first part of this book show, more areas of the library, beyond acquisition, need special attention to deliver quality services: specifically, well-trained professional personnel and an adequate technological infrastructure. This is due, not least, to the constant, rapid, technological changes, but also to changes in educational and research practices, to changed student and faculty expectations, and to changed expectations posed to graduates for life and ministry in an information society. For these reasons, librarians are called information specialists and can help navigate a theological school toward effective research support of doctoral students.

In a best-case scenario, the librarian or a faculty member responsible for the library[6] is part of the doctoral program development process. This way, he or she can gather enough bits of information on the future program to convey it to library staff and alert them to library-related expectations. The expectations for "improving the library" are definitely there, but they are often vague, not reflected upon, and insufficiently communicated. The stories of AIU and CGTS clearly demonstrate the benefit of including the library team, or at least a liaison, in the development process as early as possible (see Principle #1). Librarians are an integral part of the educational process and want to contribute to it for the sake of quality and its missional impact. If included in doctoral studies development and operation, they share valuable expertise from

---

5. The IBTSC library in Amsterdam does not really find itself in a Majority World context. Despite its more privileged position, it nevertheless encountered similar or worse problems in serving doctoral students. Hong Kong usually also compares quite differently to less resourced theological schools in Africa, Asia or Latin America. The purpose here is not to compare contexts but to observe issues that schools and libraries face when starting doctoral programs and to learn from each other's mistakes.

6. It seems not unusual in the Majority World that the library director is not a librarian but a faculty member. Many library-related issues are decided not in the library but by the academic leadership. As long as the responsible faculty member is a person of "both worlds" and familiar with specialized library processes, this can provide a functional model for a while.

and on their own professional area that will not be as obvious to members of the academic leadership.

2. Accreditation standards. A doctoral program development process will, at an early stage, consider relevant accreditation standards, those defined by the state for its national universities, as well as applicable guidelines issued by evangelical accrediting bodies. Sometimes these include quite specific requirements concerning collections and space, as well as staff numbers and their qualifications. They also change throughout the years and need to be closely monitored. This aspect had a significant impact on the AIU (see their story) as they needed to reclassify their holdings (Principle #9) and provide professional development for their staff (Principle #12), or on CGTS who needed to significantly expand their holdings of non-English books and journals (Principle #8). Sometimes accreditation standards that concern a library are vague and insufficiently clear-cut. The library then is well advised to benchmark against (seek comparability with) similar institutions (nationally and internationally) so that the school's graduates can function effectively in worldwide competitive environments. Accreditation standards for this highest terminal degree often expect comparability with state universities, which might not always be realistic for small evangelical institutions. The purpose of these standards is to improve quality and transferability/comparability of degrees. Decision makers must be aware that cutting corners in the area of library holdings and services leads to devaluation of evangelical doctoral education.

3. A print collection will not suffice. Library development for doctoral studies is sometimes presumed by the academic administration to include primarily the purchase of additional books (see the early stages of the IBTSC story). This is quite a limited "outsiders'" perspective that reduces a library to a "storage place." While collection development plays a vital role that cannot be overestimated (see Principles #5–9), print books and a classic standardized "doctoral collection"[7] will not suffice in view of the narrow individualized doctoral topics. The story of IBTSC vividly demonstrates that a wonderful print collection is of only limited value to remote students. It takes a very dedicated effort and enormous amounts of time on the part of a librarian to make a print collection useful by scanning and emailing chapters and articles

---

7. Often such "doctoral collections" primarily include titles that seem important in Western theological schools from their longstanding experience – faculty recommend books for purchase from which they themselves benefited during their own doctoral studies in the West. While these are helpful, a balance needs to be sought to enable contextual doctoral research.

from print books and journals to students (Principle #11). Many libraries all over the world had to embrace imaginative ways during the recent pandemic to "open up" their print collections to users in spite of lockdowns and movement restrictions. A print collection becomes a resource to students and faculty only together with the relevant services that can be provided only by humans – trained librarians.

The collection development policy[8] will include specific references to the acquisition of relevant digital resources, books, journals, and dissertations (Principle #8), and mention the need to consider individual requests for resources by supervisors and by doctoral students (Principle #7). It will also be supplemented by a "Doctoral Students Services" policy that specifies ways in which Inter-Library Loan (ILL) and Document Delivery services are provided (Principle #4). Library staff will need to have the vision, attitude (compassion and intuitive thinking – along with students), and time, together with technological equipment, to deliver these services (Principle #11). They will see and open up for students the whole information universe – both digital and print, paid and freely available on the internet. This will require a well-designed webpage, reference services via email and messaging and/ or the library's virtual presence in the learning management system of the theological school where students regularly come for other courses. Librarians will not tie students to their own expertise but help students develop varied research skills and strategies (Principle #14) to be effective in their research, teaching, and ministry. One-on-one service, especially in reference assistance and information competence development, as described in the CGST story, is of great advantage to doctoral students. As traditional face-to-face possibilities shrink with remote studies, much imaginative thinking outside the box will be appreciated.

4. IT infrastructure. As collections expand to include digital resources, fruitful cooperation with the IT department is crucial. This includes not only friendly relations but even, as the AIU story demonstrates, adding an IT specialist to

---

8. Many Majority World institutions with doctoral programs have built great libraries without a collection development policy. Some have written a policy in the process of developing the library (documenting decisions that were made on the way) and some have written it after the program has been implemented for a while. Their success did not depend on a pre-formulated policy but on effective cooperation and extensive communication between faculty, library, and the doctoral program development committee. Even if there is a collection development policy, the need for communication and cooperation will remain indispensable. However, a policy helps to ensure continuity and consistency in library development, in spite of staff or leadership changes.

the library team, or specifically developing a library staff member to take over technology-related functions. Open-source library software (Koha and others are mentioned in the stories) has received special attention in Majority World theological schools because it is presumed to be "free." Even if the software package can be downloaded for free from the internet, the installation, data migration, and maintenance require a dedicated IT specialist who closely cooperates with the library.

5. Cooperation is the key! Each story emphasizes how their success in quality services for doctoral students heavily depends on partnerships and cooperation – local, national, and international (Principle #4). The AIU and SAIACS stories underline how beneficial the collaboration with faculty has been for developing a qualitative collection (Principle #3). Others emphasize the valuable input and crucial help received from Western and other librarians during the process of developing doctoral programs. The desire for partnerships is often directed toward the West because of resources and experience available there; accreditation possibilities and prestige often primarily attributed to Western institutions also play a role.[9] As the pandemic with its travel limitations has shown, local grounding is vitally important. Not least, for contextual resources.

Each story mentions participation in consortia as a great way to share resources, engage in shared collection development, get access to electronic resources, run a union catalog, and share classification work. Sometimes there are opportunities to join state-operated consortia; this often presumes state accreditation and adds some stipulations (i.e. no international members, see IBTSC story). Often personal relationships between librarians of different schools and associations facilitate these partnerships. Networking and personal interconnectedness with librarians in different places also open doors to obtain resources for students (see SAIACS story).

As doctoral education in the Majority World wins ground and matures, and serious postgraduate centers develop in various parts of the world, global engagement and bilateral cooperation or agreements are appreciated. The needs and challenges of these Majority World theological schools are similar, or at least more comparable, than with Western well-resourced institutions with larger budgets. They all engage in creativity and ingenuity for survival and

---

9. Many Majority World theological schools who now run doctoral programs were started by Western missionaries; their libraries have received financial help for development that was raised in the West. National initiatives for doctoral education that sprang up during the last 5–10 years have a harder time and face a less predictable environment.

for arranging "more with less," and this experience and knowledge is worthy to be shared. In each story, the library (and theological school) faced difficult decisions and had to consider Plan A, B, and C, and then, based on their current contextual situation, chose how to move forward. No experience can be copied, but much can be learned from the dynamics of change and transition, from mistakes made and ingenious solutions invented.[10] Each institution that starts a doctoral program will face its dilemmas. The principles outlined in the first part of this book, and the stories of the second part, will hopefully provide useful guidelines and help schools and librarians avoid the same mistakes.

6. Librarians are educators. While doctoral students can be considered merely as advanced students, not much different from other students of the institution, there is and should be a qualitative difference in treating them as developing researchers, junior colleagues, original contributors. While supervisors are aware of differing approaches as they mentor doctoral students, some library functions, for example information competence training, may need to be re-envisioned with this perspective in mind (Principle #14). Faculty and library staff will need to work hand-in-hand in this area by complementing each other's skills and mindsets by shaping students' research and thinking skills from their different backgrounds and perspectives (Principle #15). Sometimes the need for student orientation and information training becomes more obvious to librarians as they work with students from very diverse educational backgrounds. Some stories show that students who have previously studied at other institutions, been out of school for a while, and/or feel intimidated by technological advances, need special guidance. It is for the librarians (faculty are often too busy) to develop encompassing initiatives to help students gain and maintain technological and research competence (Principle #13). But faculty must also be closely involved in the training as subject specialists who can make the issues discussed directly relevant to the student's topic. Often Majority World doctoral students struggle with English as a research and writing language, so the navigation of research resources in English in all formats requires additional assistance. Several stories emphasize the benefits of library staff having earned a doctoral degree and being familiar with the research process (Principle #12). This allows planning for more effective

---

10. Even in the discussions that our group of authors had in the preparation of this document/book, many times we found ourselves exchanging experience in solving similar problems and discussing the details of enriching approaches that individual schools had taken.

information literacy interventions and is a great help in reference assistance and collection development.

7. The good old money! Librarians in each of the described theological schools cooperate with those responsible for finances, either in daily operations or even in fundraising. It is of great help if the fundraising burden is alleviated by a separate effective committee (see AIU story). Librarians must still be involved by presenting the library's real needs, through wise and appealing work with donors, and also by developing creative ways to promote library needs to interested persons while seeking out grants and donations. While the school's administration might primarily see expenditures for books, furniture, and salaries, librarians need to alert budget writers to other vital areas that require investment, such as information competence training and professional development.

As these stories from different continents emphasize, theological libraries can be of formative influence and significantly impact God's kingdom. Relevant qualitative resources are vital to support doctoral students' original research and the development of new knowledge. The librarian's/library team's queen-pin position as persons who, equipped with research and guidance skills and with the right attitude, function as connectors between humans, resources, and technology, is also not to be underestimated. Institutions in the Majority World who plan to start a doctoral program or evaluate their libraries and educational processes will benefit from considering the collective experience and best practice principles surfacing in these reports.

Appendixes

Appendix 1

Profile of Doctoral Candidates in the Majority World

Katharina Penner, EAAA Coordinator
for Library Development

There is no "typical doctoral student" when it comes to research and library-use skills. Students vary widely in their information search approaches depending on previous learning and exposure, their personal life stories, experience with schools, research and libraries, and how long they have been out of school. Still, studies focusing on researchers (defined as doctoral students, postdocs, research faculty) and their use of library and information resources continue to identify some similarities, which are useful to consider when planning and leveraging library services for postgraduate students.

There are several helpful studies on research students in general and a few on theologians in particular.[1] Most of this research has been carried out in the West, and so its findings are not directly transferrable to evangelical doctoral education in the Majority World. Nevertheless, such investigation provides useful pointers and stimulates further observation and reflection. The summary that follows is based upon insights from studies, direct engagement with doctoral students in theology, and anecdotal evidence from various parts of the world. It attempts to distill key characteristics of doctoral student's library use and research practices. These have served as discussion points in

---

1. Cf. for example: "The Value of Libraries for Research and Researchers," a RIN and RLUK report, March 2011, https://www.rluk.ac.uk/portfolio-items/the-value-of-libraries-for-research-and-researchers; Lucinda Covert-Vail and Scott Collard, "New Roles for New Times: Research Library Services for Graduate Students," Association of Research Libraries, 2012, http://www.arl.org/rtl/plan/nrnt; Danielle Cooper and Roger Schonfeld, "Supporting the Changing Research Practices of Religious Studies Scholars," Ithaka S+R, February 8, 2017, https://doi.org/10.18665/sr.294119.

formulating the principles in the first part of this book for best practices for libraries that serve doctoral students in theology in the Majority World.

Use of Research Resources

Theology students, like their counterparts in the humanities, appreciate print resources when these are available.[2] Yet the expectation is rising that the library will also provide access to relevant electronic resources accessible from students' desktops.

Many useful academic resources are available on the internet free or at low cost, which adds to convenience and ease of access. For discovery of useful resources, students usually depend on electronic search tools. With practice, they become more skilled and confident in using online resources.[3] Eventually, the internet is visited more often than academic library facilities; a library is just one among multiple options for finding and accessing information. For the less resource-rich theological library in the Majority World this is a challenge, and to remain competitive and relevant[4] it needs to identify particular value-added services with a human touch to attract doctoral students to its resources.

Usually Google and similar platforms are the first stop for students at early stages of research for reasons of ease of use and student familiarity with these platforms in daily research unrelated to academic work.[5] Google Scholar is sometimes faster (due to its automatic indexing) than other services, such as Scopus or Web of Science, in providing indexing for new research. Majority World students more often than not also don't have access to these expensive indexing databases. After initial exploration and expanding of their

---

2. Print materials are more conducive to reflection and emphasize linearity of thought (which is an important skill when constructing outlines and organizing one's own writing around a thesis statement in a logical and successive way). Print materials invite marking-up and note-taking, flipping between different sections and tracing connections among ideas.

3. This is not true for every postgraduate student. Depending on previous exposure to electronic resources, on how long students have been out of school, and on other factors, some struggle. Students may be quite proficient with smartphones and other technologies, but when it comes to catalogs, databases, and learning management systems, which are more structured and expect different forms of intuition and navigation, there are certain blocks with regard to understanding and use.

4. If libraries fail to address this trend and offer neither electronic resources nor design attractive user services, they will indeed sink into irrelevance. A doctoral-level library must focus and optimize its services, customize support for the doctoral student, and find additional ways to support research.

5. Instead of lamenting the downsides of Google (and there are many!), libraries are better advised to meet students where they are and offer training for more effective use of Google products (Search, Google Scholar, Google books, etc.).

concentric searches, doctoral students will eventually arrive at library catalogs and academic databases. Often these are not used for discovery but rather to locate and access resources found through other means. Students' ignorance of the existence and benefits of academic databases and the library's ineffective promotion of such tools may explain the minimal use of open-access or paid-for databases that librarians observe.

The types of materials that postgraduate students utilize most often are journal articles,[6] book chapters, conference proceedings, and monographs. Because of limited access to print and/or digital resources in the Majority World, and depending on the academic culture of the country's state universities, students have fewer inhibitions about employing sources that are perceived as less academic in the West, such as websites, blogs, etc. Students primarily value new research but are also grateful for guidance on established "experts in the field." Personal academic networks are important in locating new and relevant research, but at the beginning of the research process these are not yet well developed, so students rely on supervisors or peers and sometimes also on alerting services. Dissertations are very useful at the beginning of research because students need to establish the originality of the research and find their "niche." The library needs to respond to this need and seek out open-access dissertations which degree-granting institutions and other platforms are beginning to make available in open-access repositories.

Contextual factors influence information seeking and use. Students, confronted with the academic pressures of a doctorate and difficulties in obtaining the right resources, are always on the lookout for workarounds – some in this are more creative and successful than others. And some already have extensive personal libraries (print and digital). However, these are not sufficient for doctoral-level studies, so work on building personal libraries continues throughout the research process.[7] Since an individual's personal collection process can be haphazard and unsystematic (whatever one can lay one's hands on!), these resources are not always well organized or cataloged,

---

6. Usually (but not always!) articles rank highest because they supply current and controversial information, which moves forward the discussion that is intrinsic to the dissertation process. Often books/monographs rank first for students in Majority World institutions, possibly because theological journals, in print or digital format, are less accessible.

7. Other reasons for building one's personal library include: the library of the institution where they are enrolled may have insufficient resources for doctoral studies, the student's topic may be quite specialized, students study at a significant geographical distance from the library, students want to have resources to fall back on after they have graduated, and the library doesn't have an alumni plan.

and they are scattered in various formats across various platforms (because no flash drive, external disk or cloud service offers enough free space for storage).[8]

Use of Library Services

Doctoral students utilize the physical library only to a limited extent. This has many and varied causes, but sometimes it is explained by the library's scarcity of study space, the library's geographical distance for remote students, the fact that the library's user population is primarily undergraduate, or previous negative experiences with a library. However, if their needs are considered, they value the library's physical space very highly. Many Majority World doctoral students don't have personal offices or fear being "discovered" and interrupted while attempting to study there. They often are also constrained in their living conditions. So they like to use library space for quiet study if the library offers available, protected, customizable space. The physical library is also valued as a place to meet fellow-researchers and to engage in discussion with them.

Convenience as well as ease of use and access are very important factors, so any kind of service that the library offers needs to consider this. Research students are always pressed for time[9] and there is a tendency to follow the "principle of least resistance." If a print or electronic resource is not immediately available or accessible, it will likely be ignored, especially after a handful of unsuccessful attempts to retrieve, order, or access it. Previous exposure to research as well as prior experience with libraries, catalogs, and academic databases positively influence the way doctoral students search. But a lack of time is a negative factor, making their search less optimal.

A preference for using electronic sources does not imply that students are proficient and efficient in utilizing them, even though they may consider themselves to be sufficiently prepared. As they usually only intermittently can dedicate quality time to research and work on the dissertation, this fact combined with partial ignorance about efficient ways to locate materials that are not easily available, leads to frustration or anxiety over the risk of missing important information.

---

8. The Ithaka report mentions the same approach to building personal libraries for Western theologians, so it seems to be a characteristic of the discipline and not of particular contexts.

9. While this is a common phenomenon – a postgraduate theology student usually has to live in and cope with expectations from different "worlds": ministry, job, studies, family – the pressures become even more palpable when economic and political pressures in the Majority World are added.

Still, doctoral students almost always prefer to do their searches themselves. This can be explained by the narrowly defined research topics, their ever-increasing specialization in their topic, and possibly because they believe that at this stage in their academic career they ought to have become independent and self-sufficient. Depending on the stage of research, different search behaviors can be observed. At the beginning, searching is quite random and unsystematic; there is some citation chaining, that is, checking references and bibliographies of useful resources for more of the like. Searches become more organized, differentiated, and strategic at later stages, sometimes under the guidance of a supervisor, sometimes because aspects of the topic have become clearer and obvious gaps have been defined. Different strategies are used iteratively, with varying degrees of depth and precision, depending on the stage of research and information needs.

Notwithstanding their reluctance to seek assistance, students do ask for help. Usually their supervisors, faculty, and peers serve as first points of contact. Doctoral students less frequently turn for help to librarians, partly due to embarrassment at appearing deficient, partly because of an exaggerated perception of their own skills, or partly because of a less collegial relationship with library staff than with supervisor or academic faculty. Possibly the students' believe that librarians cannot be sufficiently knowledgeable about their narrowly defined subject. And they are right: a librarian won't have a ready answer, but he or she can train students on how to search with various technologies for the right sources. Graduate students value reference help, inter-library loans, and other library services. They use these more often after useful training sessions or after having had a successful experience with a competent librarian. Library staff need to build relationships with doctoral students proactively and become trusted members of their informal networks. They need to be recognizable members of the academic community, proficient in social media, available in the physical library, they need to appear (and be) competent, and become dialogue partners with doctoral students, not least by asking different questions than a supervisor typically will ask.

Many students don't know what their library can do for them. The library needs to have an aggressive and creative information campaign that promotes its ability to customize services to meet each doctoral student's needs. If digital discovery tools are the preference, then digital tutorials, chat services, and a user-friendly and information-rich website will go a long way. The library needs to make students aware of its resources and services. Often an individualized approach and astute timing are the key.

Because time is scarce, it is unlikely that doctoral students will attend general workshops or seminars offered by the library. They prefer training at the point of need, "there and then," particularly when they have a question or feel stuck. As doctoral students progress through their research, their identity and self-perception changes. They gain expertise, migrate slowly but surely from student to researcher. In order for the library to communicate effectively and bring appropriate training into the student's life, the student must be treated with respect and never in a patronizing or belittling manner, no matter what the student's existing skills, knowledge, and attitude may be.

Appendix 2

Library Networks

Pieter van Wingerden, IBTSC Librarian

A topic that was mentioned several times throughout this book in both the principles and the library narratives is that of cooperation between libraries. Every library is established to serve a certain closely defined community. In our context, libraries serve a community that is involved in theological education and research. Sometimes these communities are strictly denominational, sometimes they are associated with a specific branch of the Christian family, sometimes also with a broader scope. Our collection management profiles reflect this by outlining the choices we make in our acquisitions, choices we believe will best serve our specific community. But no matter how large our budgets, there will always be individuals from our communities who need resources that are not present in our own collections. And this is why librarians love networks!

Just as librarians are always ready to serve the needs of their patrons, a similar posture of servitude exists between librarians. It is our role to make sure that our students, faculty, and researchers have the resources they need in order to complete their studies. We believe that their research and education is an important tool for the church to build the kingdom of God. As such, providing those resources is the mission in life for many librarians. Because we know that we need our colleagues to keep our own community resourced, we realize that they need our help to keep their communities resourced.

Networks of libraries are usually organized on a regional, national, and continental level, sometimes also on a denominational level. It is essential for a library to be a member of at least one of these networks. If a national network is not available, there is usually the possibility to become a direct member of a continental network. Most of these networks will organize a (bi)annual conference where theological librarians from different kinds of libraries gather to discuss practical issues in librarianship. Sometimes these conferences are organized around a theme. Examples of such themes currently are copyright, digitization, open access, subject indexing, improving service to patrons, etc.

For many librarians, these conferences are a place of inspiration, sharing with colleagues, further learning, and professional development. The resources invested (travel costs, conference fees) in allowing the librarian to visit these conferences are very modest compared to the long-term results. Meeting colleagues from around the country or continent cements relationships that only grow stronger as they interact and help each other. These personal relationships and trustful friendships often "carry" much farther when a student needs a resource; they also pave ways for institutional agreements. Through these networks, librarians from different contexts can be of and benefit from mutual support.

The most popular expressions of this type of mutual support are mailing lists. Almost every (inter)national theological library association will have a mailing list that allows their members to keep in touch with each other. And it is these mailing lists that are the secret treasure chest of every librarian. When a patron is in need of a specific resource, we can use our networks to find out if there is a colleague in another institution, perhaps in another country, or even on another continent, that might be able to share the resource with us. Because all librarians are (or should be) incredibly service-minded, we appreciate these requests and often go the extra mile to assist our colleagues in serving their patron.

For some theological libraries, these informal networks are their primary sources of support from colleagues. In addition to this, many theological libraries will also be part of more formal networks. As we have seen in our library narratives, some of us are part of national inter-library loan networks; some of us take part in national cataloguing projects; and some of us share electronic resources with one or more other libraries. These types of cooperation activities are organized more formally, and usually require the signing of contracts or memoranda of understanding between institutions. However, before signatures are placed, a change of mentality is sometimes necessary. Everyone likes to borrow, but not everyone is immediately willing to lend! Trust is a foundational aspect to consider, and it sometimes is not easy to establish, possibly due to previous disappointments, strict administrative rules, time pressures, and other issues. In some areas of the world there might not be any success initially in negotiations on an administrative level, and so personal connections between relatives or classmates can be crucial.

Given the fact that these types of networks are so diverse in what they are trying to achieve and so useful to the mission of an individual theological library, every library will have its own constellation of networks. For some libraries it will be much more important to have international connections than for others. Some libraries depend heavily on a national inter-library loan program, while others will make exclusive use of informal mailing lists to satisfy patron needs that cannot be satisfied through their own collections. Here again, in order to ensure long-term library cooperation, an institution must think of mutuality and equity, and not attempt to cover its students' and faculty' needs by completely relying on resources of others and not investing in their own library's development. Still, what all narratives in this booklet have in common is that none of our libraries could achieve the level of service that we currently provide to our community without the formal and informal, national and international networks of which we are part. Even this booklet in your hands is the direct result of the existence of such networks. We encourage your institution and your library to investigate the networking situation in your own context. They are an essential support structure for your library to achieve its mission.

For Further Reading

ACL. *Library Guidelines for ABHE Colleges and Universities*. Cedarville: Association of Christian Librarians, 2016.

Association of College and Research Libraries. *Framework for Information Literacy for Higher Education*. Chicago: American Library Association, 2016. http://www.ala.org/acrl/standards/ilframeworkapps.

———. *Information Literacy Competency Standards For Higher Education*, 2000. http://www.ala.org/acrl/standards/informationliteracycompetency.

Badke, William. "The Framework for Information Literacy and Theological Education: Introduction to the ACRL Framework." *Theological Librarianship* 9, no. 2 (2015): 4–7. https://serials.atla.com/theolib/article/view/2392.

———. *Teaching Research Processes: The Faculty Role in the Development of Skilled Student Researchers*. 2nd ed., Enroute, 2021.

Cooper, Danielle, Roger C. Schonfeld, et al. "Supporting the Changing Research Practices of Religious Studies Scholars." Ithaka S+R, February 8, 2017. doi:10.18665/sr.294119.

Covert-Vail, Lucinda, and Scott Collard. "New Roles for New Times: Research Library Services for Graduate Students." Association of Research Libraries, 2012. https://www.arl.org/wp-content/uploads/2012/12/nrnt-grad-roles-20dec12.pdf.

Ćurić, Matina, ed. *Introduction to Theological Libraries*. The Theological Librarian's Handbook, Vol. 1. Chicago: ATLA Open Press, 2020. doi:10.31046/atlaopenpress.34.

Detar, Melody Diehl. "Theological Librarianship from a Distance." *Theological Librarianship* 8, no. 2 (2015): 11–15. doi:10.31046/tl.v8i2.390.

Dunkley, James. "Theological libraries and theological librarians in theological education." In *Summary of proceedings: Forty-fifth annual conference of the American Theological Library Association*, ed. Betty A. O'Brien: 227–231. Evanston, Ill.: American Theological Library Association, 1991.

Gale, Michael, and Carol Reekie. *ABTAPL Guidelines for Theological Libraries*. Cambridge: ABTAPL Publishing, 2008. https://abtapl.org.uk/wp-content/uploads/2017/08/GuidelinesForTheologicalLibraries2008.pdf.

Gragg, Douglas L. "Charting a Course for Information Literacy in Theological Education." *American Theological Library Association Summary of Proceedings* 58 (2004): 50–53.

ICETE. "Standards and Guidelines for Global Evangelical Theological Education, 2019." https://icete.info/wp-content/uploads/2019/04/Standards-and-Guidelines-for-Global-Evangelical-Theological-Education-2019.pdf.

International Federation of Library Associations and Institutions Section on Acquisition and Collection Development. "Guidelines for a Collection Development Policy Using the Conspectus Model," 2001. https://www.ifla.org/publications/guidelines-for-a-collection-development-policy-using-the-conspectus-model.

Mayer, Robert J. "Theological Librarians and Collection Management: Collaborative Policy Development." *Theological Librarianship* 11, no. 2 (Oct 2018). doi:10.31046/tl.v11i2.530.

McMahon, Melody Layton, and David R. Stewart, eds. *A Broadening Conversation: Classic Readings in Theological Librarianship*. Lanham: Scarecrow Press, 2006. doi:10.31046/atlapress.27.

Research Libraries UK. "The Value of Libraries for Research and Researchers." A RIN and RLUK report, March 2011. https://www.rluk.ac.uk/wp-content/uploads/2014/02/Value-of-Libraries-report.pdf.

Shaw, Ian J., Scott Cunningham, and Bernhard Ott. *Best Practice Guidelines for Doctoral Programs*. Carlisle: Langham Global Library, 2015.

Smiley, Bobby, ed. *Information Literacy and Theological Librarianship: Theory & Praxis*. Chicago: ATLA Open Press, 2019. doi:10.31046/atlaopenpress.33.

Whipple, Caroline. "Collection Development in a Theological Research Library." In *A Broadening Conversation: Classic Readings in Theological Librarianship*, edited by Melody Layton McMahon and David R. Stewart. Lanham, MD: Scarecrow Press, 2006. Republished in 2019 as an eBook by the American Theological Library Association. doi:10.31046/atlapress.27.

Contributors

David Baer is Professor of Old Testament and Biblical Languages at the Biblical Seminary of Colombia. He also directs the Theological Education Initiative and serves as a visiting faculty member of the Arab Baptist Theological Seminary, Beirut, Lebanon. David has invested his adult life in theological education and organizational leadership, having served as President of Costa Rica's ESEPA Seminary and of the Overseas Council. He holds a PhD from the University of Cambridge, an MDiv from Gordon-Conwell Theological Seminary, and a BA from Wheaton College, USA.

Steve Chang (PhD, Aberdeen) is Professor of New Testament and Director of the PhD Program at Torch Trinity Graduate University in Seoul, Korea. He currently serves as co-chair of the Doctoral Initiatives Steering Committee of ICETE. He is contributor to *A Hybrid World: Diaspora, Hybridity, and Missio Dei* (2020) and *Scattered and Gathered: A Global Compendium of Diaspora Missiology* (2020).

Melody Mazuk has served as a theological librarian and theological library consultant for many years in wonderful and varied places. In theological librarianship she found the perfect meeting of vocation (librarianship) and avocation (theology). She studied at Baylor University, the University of Pittsburgh, IBTS (Rüschlikon), and Eastern Seminary. In addition to her work as a theological librarian she also served as a peer accreditor for both the Association of Theological Schools in the US and Canada and the Commission on Higher Education / Middle States Association, and as a member of the Commission on Accrediting (ATS) and a Board Member for the American Theological Library Association.

Ephraim Mudave is the University Librarian at Africa International University in Nairobi, Kenya, where he is a member of the University Management Board and the University Senate. He is a peer reviewer with the Commission for University Education in Kenya on library matters and the Patron of the Christian Association of Librarians in Africa-Kenya. Ephraim has worked in theological libraries for more than twenty-six years, mostly in management positions. He also teaches as a part-time lecturer. He has a PhD in Information Studies from the University of Kwazulu-Natal South Africa, an MA in Mission

Studies from Africa International University, a Master of Library Science from Indiana University, Bloomington, and a BSc in Information Sciences from Moi University, Kenya.

Katharina Penner was born in Soviet Kyrgyzstan and lives in Vienna. She holds two Masters degrees – one in Theology and one in Library and Information studies – and is working toward a PhD degree in Theological Education. For the past thirty years she has worked at theological schools in St. Petersburg, Russia, Prague, Czech Republic, and in Austria, as faculty member as well as library director. Since 2016 she has served as Coordinator for Library Development at the Eurasian Accrediting Association and is involved in several writing projects as an author and as a coordinator.

Yesan Sellan is Chief Librarian at South Asia Institute of Advanced Christian Studies (SAIACS), which offers postgraduate and doctoral programs in biblical and theological studies and missiology. Prior to joining SAIACS, he was librarian at Serampore College, India. Dr. Sellan holds a PhD in Library and Information Science from Bharathidasan University, Tiruchirappalli, India. He was Secretary to Forum of Asian Theological Librarians (ForATL) and currently serves as Executive Secretary to the Indian Theological Library Association (ITLA). Dr. Sellan has published widely, facilitated numerous workshops, and attended and presented papers at international conferences held in United States of America, Canada, South Korea, Thailand, Nepal, Indonesia and Singapore.

Joyce Wai-Lan Sun is an Associate Professor at the China Graduate School of Theology (CGST) in Hong Kong. She obtained her PhD in New Testament Studies from the University of Edinburgh, UK, and is the author of *This Is True Grace: The Shaping of Social Behavioural Instructions by Theology in 1 Peter.* She also served as the Librarian of CGST from 2013 to 2021.

Pieter van Wingerden is the Librarian at IBTS Centre Amsterdam, a collaborative partner of the Faculty of Religion and Theology of the Vrije Universiteit Amsterdam. Pieter holds a Master's degree in Greek and Latin Languages and Cultures, served with his wife, Hanna-Ruth, in Central Asia from 2010 to 2014, and has been in his current position since 2014. In his spare time he is studying for a PhD at Leiden University. As a librarian, it is Pieter's mission to provide the community of researchers and research students associated with IBTS Centre Amsterdam with (online) access to the required library resources.

Global Hub for Evangelical Theological Education

ICETE is a global community, sponsored by nine regional networks of theological schools, to enable international interaction and collaboration among all those engaged in strengthening and developing evangelical theological education and Christian leadership development worldwide.

The purpose of ICETE is:
1. To promote the enhancement of evangelical theological education worldwide.
2. To serve as a forum for interaction, partnership and collaboration among those involved in evangelical theological education and leadership development, for mutual assistance, stimulation and enrichment.
3. To provide networking and support services for regional associations of evangelical theological schools worldwide.
4. To facilitate among these bodies the advancement of their services to evangelical theological education within their regions.

Sponsoring associations include:
Africa: Association for Christian Theological Education in Africa (ACTEA)

Asia: Asia Theological Association (ATA)

Caribbean: Caribbean Evangelical Theological Association (CETA)

Europe: European Evangelical Accrediting Association (EEAA)

Euro-Asia: Euro-Asian Accrediting Association (E-AAA)

Latin America: Association for Evangelical Theological Education in Latin America (AETAL)

Middle East and North Africa: Middle East Association for Theological Education (MEATE)

North America: Association for Biblical Higher Education (ABHE)

South Pacific: South Pacific Association of Evangelical Colleges (SPAEC)

www.icete-edu.org